Living God's Dream

Dismantling Racism for Children

Leader Guide

Sally Ulrey, Katie McRee, and Malinda Shamburger

The Diocese of Atlanta
In collaboration with the Absalom Jones Center for Racial Healing

Copyright ©2024 the Diocese of Atlanta and Sally Ulrey, Katie McRee, and Malinda Shamburger

All rights reserved. Except for pages that are marked with permission to reproduce, no part of this book may be reproduced in any form without permission in writing from the publisher.

All scripture quotations, unless otherwise indicated, are taken from the Holy Bible New International Version®. Copyright © 1973, 1978, 1984 International Bible Society. Used by permission of Zondervan Publishing House. All rights reserved. The "NIV" and "New International Version" trademarks are registered in the United States Patent and Trademark Office by International Bible Society. Use of either trademark requires permission of International Bible Society.

Scripture quotations marked (NRSV) are from the New Revised Standard Version Bible, copyright © 1989 National Council of the Churches of Christ in the United States of America. Used by permission. All rights reserved worldwide.

The Episcopal Diocese of Atlanta www.episcopalatlanta.org
The Absalom Jones Center for Racial Healing
www.centerforracialhealing.org

Church Publishing
19 East 34th Street
New York, NY 10016
www.churchpublishing.org

Typesetting by Nord Compo
Cover design by: Ink Splatter Design

ISBN: 978-1-64065-682-6
eISBN: 978-1-64065-683-3

Library of Congress Control Number: 2024930706

Table of Contents

Foreword v

Preparation Notes 1

Lesson 1: I Am Beloved 5

Lesson 2: I Am Brave 31

Lesson/Day 3: I Am Compassionate 79

Lesson/Day 4: I Am Resistant 123

Lesson/Day 5: I Am Ready 155

Wrap-Up 183

Foreword

I am delighted to introduce *Living God's Dream: Dismantling Racism for Children*, because I believe that the process of combating systemic racism must begin as early in a child's development as possible. We must continually seek to find ways to destabilize and derail the forces of racism that work daily to divide us as God's precious children.

Our children come to earth with no reason not to believe that everyone is a precious child of the good Creator. Inevitably, they will encounter mean-spirited energy that is set in motion when difference is portrayed as a negative instead of as an example of God's creative imagination. It is difficult to understand the purpose of this negativity. The denigration of difference makes no sense when you look closely at the vast amount of beauty displayed in the many ways that it appears throughout the entire universe, through animals, plants, geography and more.

It is imperative to begin as early as possible teaching our children to value everyone as God's special creation and to see that God lives in us; and as we encounter one another, we encounter God, whose deepest dream is that we learn to live together as people who care about one another. This curriculum provides those who must care for the development of these precious little ones with a fun-filled way to guide children just beginning to interact socially onto a lifelong path that will lead to health and wellness for them as individuals and collectively for the planet with all other living things.

The planet needs us all to take a deep breath as we engage with the fact that we cannot sustain the violent, divisive world that we have allowed to develop because we have been too accommodating to the negative voices and powers among us. Scripture teaches us that we should pay attention to the voices of the children because they will help us in hearing truth that can help to set us free. We must free each other. To do so, we will have to unravel the threads of oppression and the many ways in which we obstruct the quality of life of many of God's children.

This curriculum will show children that love is stronger than hate and that telling the truth is better than hiding under the weight of falsehoods, whether in one's personal life or the collective community's history. Children will also see the value in always being kind and learn to care about their neighbors regardless of the color of their skin, the language they speak, or the food they eat. Perhaps most importantly, this curriculum will teach children to listen to their own hearts more carefully and to trust that being kind is one of the best gifts that be given to another human being.

Living God's Dream: Dismantling Racism for Children is one more step in the continual effort to make brave space where the truth can be told, and the Spirit can be free to dwell in these young souls as they help us all to see God's Dream more clearly.

Catherine Meeks, Ph.D.
Founding Executive Director of the Absalom Jones Episcopal Center for Racial Healing

Preparation Notes

We believe following Jesus is a lifelong commitment to justice, to becoming a beloved community, and to dismantling racism. The Episcopal Church, in particular, has a Baptismal Covenant that affirms we will "seek and serve Christ in all persons," that we will "strive for justice and peace among all people, and respect the dignity of every human being" (Book of Common Prayer, pages 304-305). The aim of this curriculum is to help us, especially our children, live into that dream for a world that sees the belovedness of every person, seeks to celebrate racial diversity and differences as gifts from God, and inspires us to act when the world is not living up to God's dream.

Formats

This format can be used as a 5-day VBS, or it can be used as a whole year curriculum.

VBS. The content of each lesson includes Scripture, a storybook suggestion, a personal story suggestion, music, crafts, snacks, games, and a way for children to serve. This could be set up as centers, which children rotate through, like at VBS. The repeated themes for each day are included in each activity, making it easy for the Craft Leader (as an example) to pull just the craft pages for that center.

Sunday School or other. There is a lot of content in each lesson, so that can easily be broken up to use just a couple of lesson elements each time, and then the other content used at a different time. For example, one week at Sunday School, you could use the Scripture and a craft from one of the lessons, and the next week, you can use the game/activity and a storybook. If you do it this way, just read through the repeated themes for each day and make sure you re-introduce those each time. The repeated ideas for each lesson are found in each lesson element so that it's easy for leaders to find them, no matter what element they start with or pull out from that lesson.

An "Upfront Illustration" is an option included in the introduction to each lesson. This is something that can be used in the VBS format when everyone is gathered together for the opening session. The upfront illustration can introduce the day's themes, and usually relies on a few volunteers to interact in front of the large group (with a large group, it may not be feasible for EVERYONE to interact with the illustration/props/skits, etc.) The Upfront Illustration can easily be adapted for smaller groups using this as a regular offering as well.

Living God's Dream

Lesson Elements

The content of each lesson includes Scripture, storybook suggestions, a personal story suggestion, music, crafts, snacks, games, and a way for children to serve. The elements can stand alone or be used together for a more in-depth conversation. Things to pay particular attention to in each element:

- Music: you can make up choreography to the music, as children like to move, or you can have the children help you do this, or you can just have the children move freely in the way that seems best to them, asking them if their movements have meanings. Sometimes, we have suggestions for movements, and some songs already have choreography you can look up, but this element of the lesson is less performance based (as there is not a right way to move), and more about moving freely as the Spirit moves us.
- Storybooks: There are multiple storybook options for each lesson, which will allow you to choose the ones that fit best for your group. While you can look up videos of these stories being read online, particularly for planning purposes, we encourage you to purchase the books and support the authors. If you can purchase them from places that support Black or other minority-owned businesses, that's an added bonus!
- Personal Stories: Visit the Diocese of Atlanta website (under Resources>Education & Formation, then click on the Dismantling Racism Curriculum link) to see examples of personal stories that can help learners understand how these ideas apply to real life. You might also consider having an adult leader tell a personal story on the topic.

Service Project

We encourage you to set up a service project at the beginning of the lesson series that children and families can contribute to throughout the series. The one we've noted in the curriculum has to do with refugee resettlement (see Lesson 5-Serve/Do), because there are several elements in the curriculum that encourage children to look at refugees with compassion. As leaders, you can use the example in the curriculum and/or create additional ones that fit your context.

Preparing Leaders

The content of the curriculum is intended to be the first steps of preparing our children for a lifelong commitment to dismantling racism. The materials and content are age appropriate, but there will likely be many children and families who will be brand new to these conversations and may still find some of the elements challenging. Some of the ways you can prepare your leaders to embrace the challenge might include:

- Sharing with them your hopes for the course.
- Coaching them on how to respond to sensitive questions and comments from children and possibly their parents.

- Providing them with an avenue to ask questions and share concerns with the leadership, as this will likely be a time of learning for them as well.
- Asking them to attend the parent meeting so they understand the lens in which the parents are viewing the lessons.
- Providing additional materials for personal education if desired.

Logistical preparations: if done in a VBS style, we know that the leader in the Art station, for example, may not read through everything in the whole lesson, so we've tried to put all the themes in the art lesson, and everything that leader might need right in that portion of the lesson. This may feel repetitive, but it's so that each leader has what they need on their pages, and also, we know children learn through repetition!

Parents & Caregivers

Often parents/caregivers will have questions around dismantling racism. We value transparency and partnership with parents and caregivers. While you may or may not have a formal "parent meeting," some of the things you'll want to cover with the children's grown-ups are the themes of the lessons and the intention of the curriculum: to bring to life God's dream and intention in creation (that we are all beloved parts of the human family). You can do this through a formal "Parent Meeting," an "Open House" at the start of Sunday School, or a brochure. If you are doing some kind of meeting, you might also plan to address some concerns parents and care-givers might have around the subject of race.

- Guilt/Shame: We have found that parents and caregivers are often concerned that their child may feel guilty or bad about being a member of their race. You might reassure them that the lessons reinforce that we are ALL beloved of God and created in God's image, and diversity is a beautiful part of God's plan. The curriculum does note that the world is not currently as God intended, and there are some messes we've made, and relationships that have been damaged. The curriculum acknowledges this and invites us all to partner with God in putting the world back together according to God's dream.
- CRT: Sometimes parents and caregivers wonder about Critical Race Theory (CRT). Because of the manner in which it has often been covered in the news, they may misunderstand what CRT actually is (which concerns legal theories around anti-discrimination laws typically taught in graduate-level courses, not children's curriculum). What parents/caregivers are often wondering may be whether the children will be made to feel bad about their race, particularly if they are White. You might reassure them on this point as well (see above), and also note that we won't shy away from the things that have happened in history, because understanding them helps us to know how to partner with God to put the world back together. You can also acknowledge that we know that children did nothing to cause any of the messes the world is in… they are obviously too young to

have created that! There ARE still messes in this world, though, and there is still work to be done. God still invites us to partner with God to make the world a better, more loving place, and THAT is the point of this curriculum: that we are creating a Beloved Community, where all are loved and valued. That kind of community doesn't totally exist yet in the world, and so that's what we're working on: bringing God's Dream to life! Children have a part in making the world better and more loving to all!

Lesson 1: I Am Beloved

OVERVIEW
- Theme: Creation & Diversity
- Main Idea: Racial diversity is beautiful.
- Explanation/Teaching Approach: Recognizing and celebrating the beautiful image of God in everyone and recognizing that the gifts our differences bring are key to bringing God's dream to life. We will represent this today with a collaborative quilt, where each person decorates one square, and the whole thing is even more beautiful, but wouldn't be so without the other pieces. We will also practice it by telling others the qualities of God we see in them through the candle activity described below under the Serve/Do section

Objectives:
- To understand what it means to be made in the image of God (that every human has goodness, and that goodness shows us something about what God is like) by noticing and articulating their own unique good qualities.
- To value racial diversity as beautiful and intended by God, and to value the gifts every person brings through their uniqueness by noticing differences and articulating how differences are needed, particularly through team building activities.
- To practice looking for the image of God, the goodness, in each person by telling others what good qualities they notice, particularly through the candle activity.

Elements:
1. Bible: Genesis & Revelation (which show us God's dream, God's original intention in creation, and God's ultimate fulfillment of that dream in Revelation)
2. Storybook Ideas: *God's Dream* by Desmond Tutu
3. Personal Story: Sharing about a time when "we were better together," when the diverse gifts of a community were valuable and lifegiving and could do more than one person alone.
4. Art: Make a quilt where everyone decorates their own square, and together it makes something even more beautiful.
5. Music: "Don't forget to remember" by Ellie Holcomb and "Your Beloved" by Brent Helming

6. Play/Activity: Team building activities and debriefing about how we need each other, and all our gifts are important
7. Snack: Fruit Salad (different mix, representing the differences and beauty and goodness of diversity)
8. Serve/Do: Candle activity (tell everyone the good qualities you see that they have with strips of colored tissue paper, representing different attributes)

Introduction to the Lesson and Theme

Theme: Creation & Diversity
Main Idea: Racial Diversity is beautiful.

Human beings, EVERY human being, is made in God's image. Each individual human can show us something about who God is, but we need ALL human beings to get a clearer picture of who God is. God's attributes could not be contained in just one person. We need ALL people to see more of the whole picture of who God is. *(Show puzzle here, if using the upfront illustration).* Our uniqueness is beautiful. The diversity and variety in creation and in human beings are what reveal to us more about God. Recognizing and celebrating what makes us unique as beautiful is key to seeing God's image in each person.

We will represent this today with a collaborative quilt, where each person decorates one square, and the whole thing is even more beautiful, but wouldn't be so without the other pieces, and would be incomplete. We will also practice seeing the image of God in others by telling others the qualities of God we see in them through the (flameless) votive candle holder activity.

Repeated Ideas:
- Every human being is made in God's image, which means each person has something good, and that goodness shows us something about what God is like.
- Racial differences in human beings are intended by God, and they are beautiful. Without all of humanity, we wouldn't see the whole picture of who God is.
- It is important to practice seeing the image of God in others.
- Everyone has gifts, and our differences teach us something about the world.
- We need each other and the different gifts we all bring to the table.

Upfront illustration: Puzzle

Two options:
1. For larger groups. A few children can interact with the puzzle but do it in front of the group so everyone can participate by watching the action. Get a 1000-piece puzzle and put it all together. Take out 10 or so pieces (not next to each other, so it's easy for children to see which pieces go where) and hand them out to a few children as they arrive. When you talk about how we need every human being to give us a clearer picture of who

God is, show the puzzle, which is almost complete but has missing pieces, so we can't see the picture as clear as was intended. Talk about how we are all like an individual puzzle piece (colorful, unique, cool shape, interesting), and each piece is cool and shows something neat, but we need all the pieces together to see the whole picture. And when we aren't paying attention to each unique individual and looking for the goodness God put in them, then we are missing something they have to offer to us. Invite the children with puzzle pieces to come up and help complete the puzzle by putting in the missing pieces. Explain that when we look at human beings and see the goodness God put in them, it makes our picture of what God is like become clearer.
2. For smaller groups. Everyone can interact with the puzzle. Get a puzzle of about the same number of participants (if you have a dozen kids, get a puzzle with 12 pieces), and have everyone work together to put it together. Explain as above.

LEADER TIP: For our purposes in this curriculum, when we talk about differences and diversity, we are specifically talking about racial differences, like skin color. Part of God's design in creation was diversity of races, which we see in the picture of heaven from Revelation. Those differences were intended by God and show God's creativity, and they are beautiful. The sin of racism leads people to believe that these differences are a bad thing. The goal of this curriculum is to offer children a different approach. We were not all intended to be the same race; instead, we can celebrate the beauty of human racial diversity. While racial and some other differences—such as disabilities—may require a more nuanced understanding, for our conversation in this curriculum, we refer to specific racial differences as part of God's beautiful design for creation. If children ask about differences around things like disabilities, they deserve honest answers and robust conversation. All differences teach us things we didn't know about the world. We need each other, and understanding each person's unique gifts, experiences, and perspectives help us to be our best selves. Every human being is created in God's image, and we can see the image of God in each other.

Bible Story 1 | God's Dream: Genesis & Revelation

Scripture Reference: Genesis 1:27-28, Revelation 7:9 (NRSV)

"So God created humankind in his image, in the image of God he created them; male and female he created them. God blessed them…" —Genesis 1:27-28

"After this I looked, and there was a great multitude that no one could count, from every nation, from all tribes and peoples and languages, standing before the throne and before the Lamb, robed in white, with palm branches in their hands." —Rev. 7:9

Supplies:
- Crayons or Markers
- Paper or coloring sheets
- A large poster or piece of butcher paper

Overview for Leader: The goal of this Bible lesson is to help the children see that all of God's children come together to create a clearer picture of who God is. Each person has beautiful elements that are lovely on their own, but no one person can fully reflect the vast beauty of God. The things that make us different can be a way for us to see God in each other. We need ALL of God's people to see ALL the beauty of God! We will create art to reflect God's dream for us all to live together in harmony, celebrating each other's unique qualities, creating a full picture of God's love and beauty.

Repeated Ideas from Lesson 1 "I Am Beloved":
- Every human being is made in God's image, which means each person has something good, and that goodness shows us something about what God is like.
- Racial differences in human beings are intended by God, and they are beautiful.
- Without all of humanity, we wouldn't see the whole picture of who God is.
- It is important to practice seeing the image of God in others.
- Everyone has gifts, and our differences teach us something about the world.
- We need each other and the different gifts we all bring to the table.

Storytelling Technique: Coloring God's Dream
One of the focuses for today is to help the children understand that God made us all differently with intention and that when we all come together, we get a clearer picture of God's beauty. The depth of the conversation you will be able to enter will depend on the

age of the children. For that reason, we have multiple suggestions of how to approach this conversation.

Option 1: Pre-K/Younger Elementary Age:
- Spend some time reading and discussing the scripture reference for the day, focusing on the elements that describe the beauty of God's creation, specifically the beauty of humans! There are many main ideas listed below, but a few you may want to focus on include:
  - Human beings are God's most beautiful creation.
  - We have been made in the image of God, which means you can learn about who God is by looking at the good parts of humans.
  - God has so many good things, and each of us carry at least a few of them within us: things like being loving, kind, gentle, comforting, strong, wise, good, patient, joyful, creative, and intelligent.
  - God's dream is for all of us to come together, so that we can see more clearly the beauty of God.
- After talking through the meaning of the scripture, pass out the paper or coloring sheets and crayons. Ask the kids to draw a picture of what they think God's dream would look like.
- When they are done coloring, give them some time to share their drawings with the group and invite discussion through "Wondering" Questions (listed below).

Option 2: Upper Elementary:
- Just as you did with the younger children, spend some time reading and discussing the scripture reference for the day. The older children will be able to think a bit deeper about the concept, but we will invite them to do an activity to illustrate those truths. To prepare them for the activity, you will want to focus on these main ideas:
  - Human beings are God's most beautiful creation.
  - We know what God is like because of two ways: (1) the Bible talks about what God is like, and (2) people show us what God is like… the goodness in people…that's the image of God! People can be so wonderful, and when they are wonderful, they are reflecting something about God, so we can know more about what God is like!
  - Here are some things we know about God (or ask them to think about what God is like and record on a flip chart): God is loving, kind, gentle, comforting, strong, wise, good, patient, joyful, creative, and intelligent.
- After you have discussed those ideas, invite each child to choose ONE crayon that they really like.
- Now pass out paper or coloring sheets and invite the children to draw a picture of what they think God's dream would look like. Do NOT give them any extra crayons.

- When they are done coloring, invite them to share their drawings and talk about their experience. More than likely, everyone will express some frustration with only having a single crayon to create God's dream.
- This will be a good time to talk about another important piece of how people show us what God is like. Take some time to talk through some of these main ideas and invite them to think through a few "Wondering Questions":
  - God created lots of different kinds of human beings. Lots of skin colors, eye colors, hair colors, and different heights and languages and personalities. People whose brains work in different ways. People who have different abilities and different talents. So many!
  - A lot of times, the ways we are DIFFERENT show us something about God. I know sometimes we like to all try to be the same as each other, but sometimes it's the differences that show us a little glimmer of what God is like! God created differences on purpose! Differences are so beautiful!
  - Just like having a single crayon won't allow for a complete picture, having only one type of person won't allow us to see the completeness of God's beauty.
  - "Wondering" Questions: I wonder if you can find the thing that is like God in you? I wonder if you see the thing that is like God in the friend sitting next to you? Maybe their kindness? Maybe their love? Maybe when they comforted someone? How friendly they are when they smile? How joyful they are? The way they can solve problems? The way they know so much? How creative they are? When we create things (like make art or jokes or stories or comic books), we are showing the part of us that is made in God's image, because God created everything!
- Now, invite all the children to take their single crayons and make a bigger picture together on the poster or piece of butcher paper. If they would like to add extra colors, they may… after all, there are so many types of people in the world that are not currently represented in the room!
- After they have had some time to color together, take time once again to make observations, point them back to the main ideas, and invite "wondering" questions.
  - Imagine how boring life would be if we only had one color of crayon to use! It's the variety of crayons that makes things much more beautiful and interesting, and that's the same way with human beings. Life would be so boring if there were only one kind of human, and we were all the same. It's the different kinds of humans that make life so beautiful and interesting!
  - In heaven, every different kind of human being will be there, from all over the world!!
  - This was God's dream when God created everything…that humans would fill the earth with all our diversity, and that we would see that each person shows us something about God, so we need each and every person to help us learn what God is like. Nobody is perfect, but there is something inside every single person that God gave to show us what God is like.

"Wondering" Questions:
- I wonder if you can find the thing that is like God in you? I wonder if you see the thing that is like God in the friend sitting next to you? Maybe their kindness? Maybe their love? Maybe when they comforted someone? How friendly they are when they smile? How joyful they are? The way they can solve problems? The way they know so much? How creative they are? When we create things (like make art or jokes or stories or comic books), we are showing the part of us that is made in God's image, because God created everything!
- I wonder what it will be like in heaven with all those different kinds of people from all over the world. I wonder how we'll communicate. I wonder how we'll show each other that we love each other in heaven. I wonder what we'll learn about each other and about God that we didn't know?

Summary Statement (summarize main idea of lesson & connect back to theme):
We need each other to help us see what God is like. The more people we meet, the more clear the picture of what God is like gets! It's like adding another piece to the puzzle. It's so important to look for the image of God in each person! Every person is beautiful in some way. And we need every person to help us understand more and more what God is like.

Story Book 1 | *God's Dream* by Desmond Tutu (elementary)

Overview for Leader: This story has beautiful and simple illustrations and words to show what God dreamed for the world, what God intended for creation.

Repeated Ideas from Lesson 1 "I Am Beloved":
- Every human being is made in God's image, which means each person has something good, and that goodness shows us something about what God is like.
- Racial differences in human beings are intended by God, and they are beautiful.
- Without all of humanity, we wouldn't see the whole picture of who God is.
- It is important to practice seeing the image of God in others.
- Everyone has gifts, and our differences teach us something about the world.
- We need each other and the different gifts we all bring to the table.

Introductory Statement: In our Bible verses today, we learned that God had a dream when God created everything. God created us all different, each in the image of God, each having something that shows what God is like. God's dream was for us to see God in every human being. God's dream for heaven is that we all come together from all over the world and love God and each other. Let's think a little bit more about what God's Dream for us might be.

Read the Story: *God's Dream* by Archbishop Desmond Tutu and Douglas Carlton Abrams, illustrated by LeUyen Pham, Candlewick Press, 2010.

"Wondering" Questions:
- I wonder what part of God's dream you liked the best?
- I wonder if you've helped God's dream come true in any of those ways in the book?
- I wonder how you can help God's dream come true today?

Summary Statement (summarize main idea of story & connect back to theme):
God's dream is really beautiful! Heaven is what it will be like when God's dream of us loving God and each other is all the way true. It's not all the way true right now on earth. And now we know some ways we can help God's dream come true!

Let's say the Lord's Prayer together, because it asks God to help us bring heaven (God's dream) to earth.

Personal Story 1

Overview for Leader: Sharing a personal story helps children see what these ideas might look like in real life and helps them imagine what they can do in their own lives. Lesson 1's personal story is intended to be about when the story-sharer experienced diversity as beautiful, or a story about how a group was "better together," how one person alone could not have done it as well as the group, team, or community.

Repeated Ideas from Lesson 1 "I Am Beloved":
- Every human being is made in God's image, which means each person has something good, and that goodness shows us something about what God is like.
- Racial differences in human beings are intended by God, and they are beautiful.
- Without all of humanity, we wouldn't see the whole picture of who God is.
- It is important to practice seeing the image of God in others.
- Everyone has gifts, and our differences teach us something about the world.
- We need each other and the different gifts we all bring to the table.

Introductory Statement: We are all different. As we read in our scripture lesson, God created the world and everything in it. When God created people, God made them all unique. Sometimes, we feel that we are not special, and there are times when people say things that are not nice about us and we forget how special we are to God. God created us special, and our differences can be such a gift! We need each other!

Share a story
Check out examples of stories you could share showing how these themes look in real life by visiting the Diocese of Atlanta website (under Resources>Education & Formation, click the link for the Dismantling Racism curriculum), or have a leader share a story of their own. You could share a story on the theme of the beauty of diversity by sharing about a time when you realized how wonderful and beautiful diversity is, and how you saw the image of God in another person who was different from you in some way. Or you could share a story on the theme of how we are "better together" (like the puzzle piece illustration or the quilt we'll end up making) and how valuable and lifegiving community is in your life.

Summary Statement (summarize main idea of story & connect back to theme):
When God created flowers, God made them all different. We have red, purple, yellow, and many other colors, and God said, "This is good." Just like there are many different flowers, God created many different people, and God said, "This is very good." We are beloved by God.

Art 1 | Quilt

Supplies:
- Fabric squares of all different colors
- Strips of fabric
- Buttons
- Fabric puff paint
- Sharpies

Overview for Leader: The children will make a quilt, each of them creating their own square which reflects the unique beauty and goodness God created them with as individuals. When the quilt is sewn together, it will show that we can create something more beautiful when we come together as one. We are each beautiful in our own way and even more beautiful together. God has connected us, and together we reflect God's beauty and diversity. The quilt will be created during this lesson and will be displayed at the end of the lesson series as a reminder.

Repeated Ideas from Lesson 1 "I Am Beloved":
- Every human being is made in God's image, which means each person has something good, and that goodness shows us something about what God is like.
- Racial differences in human beings are intended by God, and they are beautiful.
- Without all of humanity, we wouldn't see the whole picture of who God is.
- It is important to practice seeing the image of God in others.
- Everyone has gifts, and our differences teach us something about the world.
- We need each other and the different gifts we all bring to the table.

Introductory Statement: Today, we're going to do an art project that shows (1) that each individual is unique and beautiful and has been made in God's image with goodness, and (2) that when we are connected together in a community, something even more beautiful is made! We need each other!

Instructions:
- Pass out squares of fabric to each person.
- Instruct them to decorate their square to show some of their good (God) qualities, their talents, their passions, their personality traits, things they like, things they're good at, etc. (These don't have to be pictures; they can be symbols…like a yellow button can symbolize the sun and their sunny personality.)
- Give them items to decorate their square (fabric markers, other strips of fabric they can cut and glue on their square with fabric glue, buttons, puff paint, etc.)

- When they are finished, have them share their square and what it says about them with the group.
- Once everything has dried, recruit someone to put the squares together in a quilt (either sewing, or using fabric glue), even if it's just the quilt cover. You can even have someone actually attach batting, etc., and create a quilt if you want. The final product will be revealed at the end of the lesson series.

Summary Statement (summarize main idea of art & connect back to the theme):
This quilt will show that:
- Each person, like each square, is beautiful and special and unique.
- When we are being creative and creating something, we are being like God, who also is so creative and created everything!
- We need each other! Alone, each person is still special and unique, but together, it is even more beautiful, and it's a whole quilt!
- We are all connected together, just like the squares of the quilt are.

Music 1

Songs: "Don't Forget to Remember" and "Your Beloved"

Song #1: "Don't Forget to Remember" by Ellie Holcomb on the album *Sing: Remembering Songs*, released in 2020.

Overview for Leader: "Don't Forget to Remember" by Ellie Holcomb is a song that encourages us to look around at the beauty of creation, and let it be a reminder of the beauty that God also created in us. The song is based on a children's book by the same name, which could be a wonderful addition as well. (Children's book: *Don't Forget to Remember* by Ellie Holcomb, illustrated by Kayla Harren, published by B&H Kids, March 3, 2020)

Repeated Ideas from Lesson 1 "I Am Beloved":
- Every human being is made in God's image, which means each person has something good, and that goodness shows us something about what God is like.
- Racial differences in human beings are intended by God, and they are beautiful.
- Without all of humanity, we wouldn't see the whole picture of who God is.
- It is important to practice seeing the image of God in others.
- Everyone has gifts, and our differences teach us something about the world.
- We need each other and the different gifts we all bring to the table.

Introductory Statement to Singing the Song: Today we have been talking about the beauty of God's creation, specifically in us! This song reminds us that we are also a beautiful part of God's creation and that we can learn about God by paying attention to the beauty around us.

Special Instructions/Motions: You can choreograph motions to key words in the song or invite the children to help you.

Summary Statement (summarize main idea & connect back to the theme):
As we see the beauty in the world, we can also see the beauty in ourselves and in each other. We are all made in God's image, and there is something wonderful about each of us! God loves us so much. You will never look at someone who God doesn't love! Let's look for the beauty in each person, and let's remember to love each other like God loves us.

<u>**Song #2**</u>: "Your Beloved" by Brent Helming (if you have a CCLI License, it is song #1963849 ©1996 Mercy/Vineyard):

Overview for Leader: This song has to do with creation, and also that the God who created everything LOVES US! We are God's beloved. It's a little bit slow and lyrical, but sweet and pretty. If you have someone who can play it, you could speed it up a bit.

Repeated Ideas from Lesson 1 "I Am Beloved":
- Every human being is made in God's image, which means each person has something good, and that goodness shows us something about what God is like.
- Racial differences in human beings are intended by God, and they are beautiful.
- Without all of humanity, we wouldn't see the whole picture of who God is.
- It is important to practice seeing the image of God in others.
- Everyone has gifts, and our differences teach us something about the world.
- We need each other and the different gifts we all bring to the table.

Introductory Statement to Singing the Song: Today, we learned that God created all of this beautiful creation, and then God created all of us in God's image, and God loves us SO MUCH! God created us all unique with beautiful differences. And each one of us shows something about who God is. Each and every one of us is loved by God. When you're loved by someone, you are their *beloved*. So, since God loves you all, you are God's beloved. *(Pointing to different children)* You are beloved of God, you are beloved of God, you are beloved of God, you are beloved, you are beloved… each and every person in this room and in this world is beloved by God. So, we're going to sing this song to remind us that the God who is so powerful to create everything, created you and said you were beloved. And we need to remember that each and every person is beloved. You will never look at someone God doesn't love! You are all God's beloved!

Summary Statement (summarize main idea & connect back to the theme):
Every human being is made in God's image, which means each person has something good, and that goodness shows us something about what God is like. God loves every single person. It is important to remember that YOU are beloved by God, and that everything that makes you special and unique is beautiful. It is also important to practice seeing the image of God in others and all their beauty, too, because each person is loved by God as well!

Play/Activity 1

Option 1: We Need Each Other! (Team Building Activity)

Supplies:
- At least 4 articles of clothing:
  - Hat
  - Gloves
  - Sunglasses
  - Coat
  - Scarf

Overview for Leader: These activities will help illustrate that every human being is made in God's image, which means each person has something good (unique strengths, skills, and traits to offer). During these activities, children will see that every person is needed. We need each other and the different gifts, talents, and abilities we all bring to the table. The children will definitely need each other and to work together as one in order to complete these games.

Repeated Ideas from Lesson 1 "I Am Beloved":
- Every human being is made in God's image, which means each person has something good, and that goodness shows us something about what God is like.
- Racial differences in human beings are intended by God, and they are beautiful.
- Without all of humanity, we wouldn't see the whole picture of who God is.
- It is important to practice seeing the image of God in others.
- Everyone has gifts, and our differences teach us something about the world.
- We need each other and the different gifts we all bring to the table.

Introductory Statement: God created all of us different on purpose. We all have different gifts and talents, but none of us have ALL the gifts and talents, so we need each other! One person might be really good at planning things out, one person might be really good at encouraging a group to enthusiastically complete a task, one person might be really good at following instructions precisely. Because we were created with different gifts, we need each other, because one person will have a gift or talent that we don't have and that we need. And we have gifts and talents that others don't have, but they need. So together, we accomplish a lot more than alone. Today we're going to play a game where we will need EVERYONE to accomplish the task. None of us will be able to do it alone; we'll only be able to do it if we have everyone working TOGETHER.

Instructions:

- One person is the "mannequin." Working together as a Team, children must find, pick up, and put the clothes on the mannequin. If they don't get all the articles of clothing, you can just record how many they get in the allotted time period. This is challenge by choice; children can volunteer for which roles they have, and if they don't want to do it alone, they can choose a partner or a group. Options should be given for how to adjust games to help children feel comfortable playing.
- Here are the parts of the Team:
  - Planner (can't talk except to whisper in the "Speaker's" ear, and can see where all the objects are and plan out the path and instructions)
  - Speaker (the only one who can talk)
  - Doers (at least two people, linked together, must follow the Speaker's instructions)
  - Mannequin (person on whom they are putting the clothes)
  - Encouragers (who cannot talk but they can gesture enthusiastically and use non-verbal communication to encourage others)
- The Planner can see where the clothes are and whisper instructions to the Speaker. The Speaker tells the Doers where to go. Once they locate an article of clothing, the Doers pick it up, and, following the Speaker's instructions, they move to the Mannequin, where they put the article of clothing on the Mannequin.
- No one can do anything outside their role. The doers can't do anything except what the Speaker instructs; the Speaker can't say anything unless the Planner tells them to say it. The Encouragers can't say anything or pick anything up. If children really want to focus on doing just their role, they might close their eyes. For example, if the doers really want to try to listen only to what the Speaker is instructing, they might just close their eyes and try to only follow the exact instructions.

Debrief/Discussion:

What did it feel like to be the Planner...to see but not be able to talk directly? Frustrating? Easy?
What did it feel like to be the... Speaker? Doers? Mannequin? Encouragers?
What successes did you have during this activity?
What did you learn about each other's strengths?

Summary Statement (summarize main idea of activity & connect back to the theme):

We need each other. We all have different strengths and different talents and abilities. We don't all think the same way. Some of us are really good at talking. Some of us are really good at listening. We need talkers and we need listeners. We need all the kinds of people to bring God's dream to earth, to help everyone understand what God is like, to bring love to all people. We need ALL of us to do that. We can't do it alone. God has given us other human beings because we need each other!

LEADER TIP: This game requires about 4-5 people. If you have a big group and enough adults, you can do multiple groups completing this task at the same time; you'll just need to bring supplies for each group. Or you can have 4-5 children volunteer and the rest of the group can watch. Either way, this is "challenge by choice," meaning the children can decide how much of a challenge they want to take on, so children should be allowed to participate in the ways in which they feel comfortable (or not participate). Everyone who participates should volunteer after knowing what is being asked of them. If they want to, they can close their eyes. Or they don't have to and can just not do anything until the "Speaker" instructs them. If the "mannequin" doesn't want others putting articles of clothing on them, then the articles of clothing can be handed to the mannequin, who can put them on. This is about team work, and leaders can modify it as needed to honor children's preferences and comfort levels during this activity. You'll also want to pay attention to making sure everyone has a role they are comfortable with, and no one feels left out.

Option 2: Frisbee

Supplies:
- Soft frisbee

Overview for Leader: These activities will help illustrate that every human being is made in God's image, which means each person has something good (unique strengths, skills, and traits to offer). During these activities, children will see that every person is needed. We need each other and the different gifts, talents, and abilities we all bring to the table. The children will definitely need each other and to work together as one in order to complete these games.

Repeated Ideas from Lesson 1 "I Am Beloved":
- Every human being is made in God's image, which means each person has something good, and that goodness shows us something about what God is like.
- Racial differences in human beings are intended by God, and they are beautiful.
- Without all of humanity, we wouldn't see the whole picture of who God is.
- It is important to practice seeing the image of God in others.
- Everyone has gifts, and our differences teach us something about the world.
- We need each other and the different gifts we all bring to the table.

Introductory Statement: If we are going to help God's dream for the world come true and create a world where every human being is valued and loved, and we all treat each other as beloved children of God who are made in God's image, then we will have to learn to work together. We will have to learn to offer our gifts and the things we are good at, and we will have to learn to help each other when needed. We can't do it unless we do it together. In this game, you won't be able to accomplish the task unless you work together, use your strengths, and help each other if needed.

Instructions:
- Have everyone start by standing in a circle.
- Each person throws the frisbee to someone who hasn't received it yet, until everyone has had a chance to catch it and throw it (so the last person to catch will throw to the first person who threw it).
- One rule you might want to implement to make it a little bit challenging is that no one can pass to the person right next to them (the person directly to their right or left in the circle).
- The task is to get through one round where the frisbee is thrown and caught by every single person without being dropped. The group together can modify how they throw it

or catch it, how close they are to each other (so some throws might be more like passes), the order in which they throw it, where they stand in the circle, or even whether they use a circle at all in order for the throws and catches to be successful. They may even want to change the shape to accommodate the needs of the group (if the original system isn't working, they can create something new that does work, so that everyone can play).
- The point is for the group to work as a team to accommodate each other in order to accomplish the task. They can teach each other techniques, encourage each other, think of new ideas to try to help those who dropped it, invite them to come in closer so it's easier to catch, etc.

Debrief/Discussion:

We need each other, every part, to really work together and get things done. I wonder what your strengths are and what you need other people's help with. I wonder how you can use the things you're good at to help someone else. I wonder how you saw the group working together, using strengths, and helping others?

Summary Statement (summarize main idea of activity & connect back to the theme):

In this game, you couldn't accomplish the task unless everyone participated in some way, and your job was to figure out how to do it in a way that everyone needed, using people's strengths and helping others when they needed it. To help bring God's dream of the world to life, we will need everyone working together. We will need everyone's perspectives, wisdom, skills, abilities, and ideas. We will need to offer our gifts and the things we're good at, and we will need to help each other when it's needed. We need EVERYONE if we are going to help God's dream for the world come true.

LEADER TIP from Rev. Dr. Mary Grace DuPree: Some of the children that participate in these games and activities will have disabilities – hearing, visual, intellectual, or physical. Many of these disabilities (like autism or epilepsy) will not be visible to you. Sometimes children are eager to teach other children about their disability and are tired of their disability being treated like it is un-nameable. Other children will feel the opposite way and want as little attention drawn to their disability as possible – and sometimes children might feel both those impulses at once.

Be on the lookout for children whose disabilities might not be immediately apparent – the child who struggles with a particular activity might have a processing disorder, might be hard of hearing, or might have a physical disability you can't see. Don't interrogate a child about a potential disability; just quietly help, while being respectful and careful of a child's dignity. Be prepared to quickly pivot, alter, or rearrange an activity when needed. If you spot potential pitfalls about an upcoming activity and a child's ability, it's better to skip that activity altogether in favor of one that would present fewer challenges or simply move on.

Some of these games and activities ask children to voluntarily limit their physical ability. Because of that, questions might arise from children who wonder if not being able to see, or speak, or walk is a difference like race or national origin. Meet this question head-on, and acknowledge that while disability certainly is a difference, there are important distinctions. (God wills our differences, but God does not will suffering, and many children are old enough to know that disability often involves pain.) A good way to redirect their question is to ask, as Lesson 3 discusses: what do we "see" when we look through the lens of this difference? How would the world look different to us? How would the world treat us differently?

Finally, keep in mind that children with disabilities are used to navigating a world that is full of challenges, and they often know their own needs well. If you see a child whose disability is (or becomes) apparent to you, don't be afraid to ask them discreetly if there's anything they need from you, or any way you can help them. If the answer is no, respect their no. Do what you can to make sure every child has the opportunity to enjoy this curriculum, while recognizing that no curriculum – or leader – is perfect.

The Rev. Dr. DuPree's field is the history of religious thought, and she has been an educator for twenty years. As a person with disability and the mother of four children with disabilities, she is excited to turn her passion for teaching to the theological conversation around accessibility justice. Rev. Dr. DuPree will be ordained to the priesthood in 2024.

Snack 1 | Fruit Salad

Supplies:
- A variety of fruits that the children would enjoy
- Knife and cutting board
- Small bowls or cups
- Spoons or forks

Overview for Leader:
A variety of fruits makes our snack and life more exciting and interesting in the same way that a variety of people adds a richness!

Repeated Ideas from Lesson 1 "I Am Beloved":
- Every human being is made in God's image, which means each person has something good, and that goodness shows us something about what God is like.
- Racial differences in human beings are intended by God, and they are beautiful.
- Without all of humanity, we wouldn't see the whole picture of who God is.
- It is important to practice seeing the image of God in others.
- Everyone has gifts, and our differences teach us something about the world.
- We need each other and the different gifts we all bring to the table.

Introductory Statement:
God has given us so many yummy fruits that taste wonderful on their own, but when we combine them into a bowl of mixed fruit, it's even more delicious! There are different colors, textures, and flavors that make the snack that much more enjoyable. In the same way, we are all special on our own, but when all of God's children come together, our unique qualities work together to provide a fuller experience of who God is.

Instructions
- Cut the fruit into bite size pieces.
- Distribute fruit into bowls/cups, making sure there is at least one piece of each type of fruit in every serving.
- Serve with a fork or spoon.
- As they are eating, talk through some of the main points from the day's lesson (see Summary Statement for help).
- Invite the children to share: What is your favorite fruit? Would you only want to eat one fruit for the rest of your life? Why is it nice to have lots of different fruits to choose from?

Summary Statement (summarize main idea & connect back to the theme):
The fruit salad is a metaphor for how we are all different, yet we all carry the goodness of God. There are so many delicious flavors and textures in fruits that they can't all fit into a single kind. Sure, you may have one that is your favorite, and you enjoy eating quite often, but it would be really unfortunate if you only had one option of fruit for your entire life! You would miss out on so much flavor and sweetness. The mixture of fruits is special because there are a greater number of flavors and textures. In the same way, God has so many good qualities that they can't all fit into a single person, so they have to be spread out over so many different types of people. One person alone is special, but when we appreciate everyone together, it's magical and makes for a clearer reflection of God!

Serve/Do 1 | Candle Encouragements

Supplies:
- One clear glass votive candleholder per child Several different colors of tissue paper, cut or torn into pieces that are about the size or a postage stamp
- Modge Podge, or some other type of glue that can be brushed on
- Brushes
- Sticky notes, note cards, or another small piece of paper.
- Flameless votive candles

Overview for Leader:
In this activity, the children will be creating votive candles for each other that represent the different qualities of God that they see in each other. Different qualities of God will be represented by various colors of tissue paper that will be glued to the outer glass of the candle, creating a stained-glass effect.

Repeated Ideas from Lesson 1 "I Am Beloved":
- Every human being is made in God's image, which means each person has something good, and that goodness shows us something about what God is like.
- Racial differences in human beings are intended by God, and they are beautiful.
- Without all of humanity, we wouldn't see the whole picture of who God is.
- It is important to practice seeing the image of God in others.
- Everyone has gifts, and our differences teach us something about the world.
- We need each other and the different gifts we all bring to the table.

Introductory Statement:
We know that God's goodness is reflected in each of us and that we all have different qualities that come from God. In this activity, we are going to practice recognizing those qualities that we see in each other. We will take time to think about how our friend's strength or creativity or other good thing is a reflection of God. And we will also celebrate how God's wonderful qualities shine in each of us.

Instructions:
- Choose several qualities of God that are also present in humans. Below is a list with scripture references that might help, but you are welcome to add your own or edit:
  - Creative: Genesis 1:1
  - Steadfast/Unchanging/Faithful: Deuteronomy 7:9

Living God's Dream

- Loving: 1 John 4:8
- Beautiful: Psalm 27:4
- Merciful: Titus 3:4-7
- Wise: Isaiah 55:9
- Patient: 2 Peter 3:9
- Strong: Psalm 46:1
- Generous: Ephesians 1:7-9
- Kind: Psalm 63:3
- Loves justice: Deuteronomy 10:18
- Gentleness: Matthew 11:29

- Make sure that you have a different color of tissue paper to represent each quality and that they are separated by color. Label them with the quality they represent.
- Place out small bowls of cups of glue and brushes.
- Prepare the candles by making sure that every child has one with their name on the BOTTOM and that the candle is placed on top of a sheet of paper with their name on it, so that other children will be able to see who it belongs to when they all start moving around.
- Remind the children that we all hold different qualities of God and that we don't all possess every single quality.
- Take some time to go over the qualities, pointing out the color that is associated with each quality. If you have time, look up and read the verses together.
- Now ask the children to think about which of these qualities they see in each other. Have them go around to other children's candles and glue on a piece of paper to represent the quality they see in their friend. Encourage them to try and think of at least one quality for each person in the room.
- Adults can also add pieces of paper, especially for children that are less well known in the group.
- If time permits, give the children the time and space to notice the qualities that their friends saw in them. Are there any surprises? Do you think they got it right? How do you feel looking at your candle and knowing how other people see you?
- Turn on the candles and close in prayer, thanking God for the ways that God is reflected in us, and asking that we would be able to notice and appreciate God's qualities in other people.

Summary Statement (summarize main idea & connect back to theme):
Take your candle home and put it somewhere where you will see it often. When you look at it, remember that it represents all the wonderful qualities that other people can see in you!

Remember that each of our candles look at least a little bit different because we all reflect God in different ways. God chose our good qualities specifically for us, and we are at our best when we can all appreciate and share those qualities freely.

Living God's Dream

Lesson 2: I Am Brave

OVERVIEW
- Theme: History
- Main Idea: I can be brave to face hard things (James Baldwin "Not everything that is faced can be changed, but nothing can be changed without being faced.")
- Explanation/Teaching Approach: When we see difference, God intended for us to be enriched, but humans often turn away from God's intention and instead see difference and treat others as "less than." We'll explore some examples including: the treatment of native peoples, Africans being enslaved, Asian and Latinx immigrants, and the doctrine of discovery. Then, we'll relate them to real life times of seeing unfairness, being left out, having an exclusive us-vs-them mentality.

Objectives:
- To understand that humans make a mess of God's dream when they treat differences with violence and fear or separation, and that bravery is required to face those messes and turn toward each other
- To value being brave to face our messes by engaging in the stories of how humans have messed up God's dream
- To practice being brave by working on building relationships

Elements:
1. Bible: Joseph and his brothers. Sometimes we might relate to Joseph (treated unfairly), and sometimes we might relate to his brothers (who treated others unfairly and needed to make amends and seek forgiveness). When we've made a mess or we're in a mess, we can be brave and face those hard things.
2. Story Book:
   a. *Brave Molly* by Brooke Boynton-Hughes
   b. *The Lion Inside* by Rachel Bright and Jim Field (for younger kids)
   c. Stories of segregation (left out), African enslavement (injustice, unfairness)
   d. Doctrine of discovery (saw difference and treated as "less than")
3. Personal Story: Story about making a mistake in a friendship but having the courage to try to fix it and make it better

4. Art: Mosaic, making something beautiful out of a mess, being brave enough to face the mess, not turn away or leave it a mess, but work on it
    a. Pottery Mosaic: smash up pottery/tiles and make something new & pretty out of it
    b. Paper mosaic: (rip up paper)
    c. Bravery medals
5. Music: "Brave" by David Dalton, John Cassetto, Jyro LaVilla, Socrates Perez, Stefanie Cassetto, Temree Miller; "Brave Enough" by Amanda Meisenheimer; "Beautiful Things" by Michael and Lisa Gungor
6. Play/Activity: Bravery Scale
7. Snack: Blue jello for Joseph in a well, and you have to dig him out
8. Serve/Do: Be brave by (list lots of options to practice at home like apologizing to someone they have hurt)

Introduction to Lesson and Theme

Theme: History

Main Idea: I can be brave to face hard things. I can reach out when I see people are separated and include them. I can face messes and help God make them beautiful. (James Baldwin-"Not everything that is faced can be changed, but nothing can be changed without being faced.")

Upfront Illustration: Messes

Have leaders act out a skit of breaking something or spilling something or making a mess. One leader will talk about how the object (a lamp, vase, jar of flour, stuffed animal, sweater, whatever it is…) is important to them and means a lot to them, and then walk away. The other leader comes in and accidentally knocks it over, spills it, rips it, etc. That leader wants to hide the mess, but decides to be brave, tell the truth, apologize, clean it up, and help make things right with the person. Talk about how if you've ever made a mess, even if it's an accident, it's easy to want to hide it, but being brave means facing it and trying to fix it. God has given us the courage we need to help face the things that are wrong with the world, and to help fix them. We're going to look at some messes today, some things that got messed up, some things that are wrong with the world, and we're going to start to think about how to help those messes.

Introduce the Main Ideas (say something like):

Have you ever made a mess? Maybe you broke something, and you had to tell a grown up about it? Sometimes it can be so scary to tell someone when you broke something or made a mess. Sometimes we want to run away and hide instead of facing the mess and trying to fix it. Fear holds us back. It takes so much courage to try to fix our messes. We have to admit when we've messed up and talk to people. We have to face it and try to fix it. We have to be brave.

Have you ever come across a huge mess that you didn't make? But it was such a big mess it was causing problems for people? Something like litter all over a highway? Even though you didn't litter, you know that litter is hurting animals and the earth, so you might want to help face that mess and fix it. It might seem too big to fix on our own, but if we're brave, we can face those messes, even ones we didn't make, and help to fix them.

When we see differences like skin color, God intended for us to be enriched, but humans often turn away from God's intention, and instead see difference and let that separate them, and even use it as an excuse to treat others as "less than." Sometimes people leave out and ignore those who seem to be different. Sometimes they treat them unfairly and are mean to them. Sometimes they think they can take what's theirs just because they're different. Human beings have done things like this lots of times and in lots of ways.

Because we have turned away from God's intention that we be enriched by differences, we have made a huge mess and have hurt each other in so many ways. We have left others out, and we have hurt others and damaged our relationships. We must be BRAVE in order to face the mess we've made.

James Baldwin saw some messes. People treated him unfairly just because of the color of his skin. James wanted to try to fix that mess, but lots of people discouraged him from trying to change anything. James Baldwin said, "Not everything that is faced can be changed, but nothing can be changed until it is faced."

There are lots of ways we have made messes. When we are mean to the earth (like with littering), that's making a physical mess. When we are mean to people or leave them out just because they're different, that's making a mess in our relationships and friendships. Human beings have made a lot of messes. We're going to learn about some ways that human beings have made some messes, mainly by being mean to each other. Sometimes they see differences and let those differences separate them, instead of coming together, seeing that we need each other. Sometimes they see differences and are really mean and even violent to each other. If we want to help fix those things, we have to be brave and face the mess! But we can do it! God says, "Be strong and courageous! Do not be afraid; do not be discouraged! The Lord your God will be with you wherever you go!" (Joshua 1:9)

So today, we're going to face some messes, so that we can help fix them. It will take courage to face the messes, and it will require us to be brave to try to fix the messes. But we can do it! Are you ready to learn about some messes and how to be brave to help fix them?

Repeated Ideas:
- God's Dream: God made us all different, and that is beautiful! God intended differences to bless us and enrich us. We need each other to see God (like the puzzle), and we need each other to be whole, full humans (like how we're all like different parts of a team).
- The mess: Humans have often looked down on differences and responded by either (1) letting differences separate us or (2) treating those who are different with unfairness. When we let differences separate us instead of bringing us together, when we treat other humans with unfairness, we mess up God's dream. We make a mess.

- Being Brave: When we see that differences have separated us, we must be brave to reach out and invite others to come together as God intended. When we see that there is a mess (hurt, people being left out, unfairness), we must be brave to face the messes and try to work on them and fix them.
- With God's help, we can help make the messes into something beautiful.

Bible Story 2 | Joseph & His Brothers

Scripture Reference: Genesis: 37, 41-45

Excerpts from Chapter 37

³ *Now Israel loved Joseph more than any of his other sons, because he had been born to him in his old age; and he made an ornate robe for him.* ⁴ *When his brothers saw that their father loved him more than any of them, they hated him and could not speak a kind word to him....*

¹⁴ *So [Jacob] said to [Joseph], "Go and see if all is well with your brothers and with the flocks, and bring word back to me."*

¹⁷ᵇ *So Joseph went after his brothers and found them near Dothan.* ¹⁸ *But they saw him in the distance, and before he reached them, they plotted to kill him.*

¹⁹ *"Here comes that dreamer!" they said to each other.* ²⁰ *"Come now, let's kill him and throw him into one of these cisterns and say that a ferocious animal devoured him. Then we'll see what comes of his dreams."*

²¹ *When Reuben heard this, he tried to rescue him from their hands. "Let's not take his life," he said.* ²² *"Don't shed any blood. Throw him into this cistern here in the wilderness, but don't lay a hand on him." Reuben said this to rescue him from them and take him back to his father.*

²⁶ *Judah said to his brothers, "What will we gain if we kill our brother and cover up his blood?* ²⁷ *Come, let's sell him to the Ishmaelites and not lay our hands on him; after all, he is our brother, our own flesh and blood." His brothers agreed.*

²⁸ *So when the Midianite merchants came by, his brothers pulled Joseph up out of the cistern and sold him for twenty shekels of silver to the Ishmaelites, who took him to Egypt.*

Overview for Leader:

This lesson is about facing the messes that we have made. The Scripture story is about a time when seeing differences caused jealousy, competition, and unfairness, and made a huge mess of the relationships between Joseph and his brothers. That was not God's dream. Joseph and his brothers had to eventually face the mess they had made, and his brothers had to repent and show changed behavior. Then, after facing the problem, telling the truth, and changing behavior, there was a chance for reconciliation and having a relationship again. When we get in a mess in our relationships, and we've been treated unfairly, or we've treated someone else unfairly, we can follow those same steps to help make it right.

Repeated Ideas for Lesson 2 "I Am Brave":

- God's Dream: God made us all different, and that is beautiful! God intended differences to bless us and enrich us. We need each other to see God (like the puzzle), and we need each other to be whole, full humans (like how we're all like different parts of a Team).
- The mess: Humans have often looked down on differences and responded by either (1) letting differences separate us or (2) treating those who are different with unfairness. When we let differences separate us instead of bringing us together, when we treat other humans with unfairness, we mess up God's dream. We make a mess.
- Being Brave: When we see that differences have separated us, we must be brave to reach out and invite others to come together as God intended. When we see that there is a mess (hurt, people being left out, unfairness), we must be brave to face the messes and try to work on them and fix them.
- With God's help, we can help make the messes into something beautiful.

Storytelling Technique: Snapshots

Tell the story (the leader can summarize, use a children's Bible, or a video of children's story). By way of a summary, the main ideas of the story are below:

Sometimes we make a mess of our relationships. Joseph was one of 12 sons. He was his father's favorite, and everyone knew it, because their father gave Joseph a special coat, which was a big deal in that time and place. His brothers were jealous, and Joseph didn't always make it easier on them. In fact, sometimes he kind of rubbed it in. He had a dream that he said meant that his brothers would bow down to him and he would be a ruler over them, and he made sure to tell them ALL about that dream. Well, one day they had enough, and plotted to kill Joseph! But the oldest brother, Reuben stood up to them (kind of) and stopped them from killing him by having him thrown into a well instead. Apparently, Reuben's plan was to go back and get Joseph out later, but before he could do that, the other brothers sold Joseph into slavery in Egypt. They told their father a wild animal had attacked Joseph, and they even tore up the coat and put some blood on it to make their lie seem convincing. Long story short, Joseph still had dreams and could interpret their meaning, so when Pharaoh, the ruler of Egypt, had a dream that no one could interpret, someone mentioned they knew a guy who was good with dreams and their meanings. So, Joseph was able to help Pharaoh understand his dream, what was going to happen (a famine was coming), and what they needed to do (store up some grain). Because of that, Pharaoh put Joseph in charge of basically everything. When the famine hit, Joseph's family didn't have food, so they went down to Egypt to buy some. They didn't recognize Joseph and bowed down to him, requesting to buy food. Joseph could have denied them help; he could have been mean to them like they were mean to him. But he didn't end up doing that. In the end, he ended up helping his family. But he did do this weird thing where he planted silver in the backpack of his youngest brother, Benjamin (his father's second favorite son), making it look like Benjamin had stolen it, the penalty for which was being enslaved. Kinda weird, but it seems like maybe that was a test to see if his brothers had changed, because Judah, the one whose idea it was to sell Joseph into slavery, said he would rather become a slave than see Benjamin be enslaved. So rather than let something bad happen to another brother, Judah appears to have changed, and would let the bad thing happen to him instead. That's a very different Judah than the one we saw earlier in the story; the one who sold one brother into slavery is now offering to be enslaved himself rather than let a different brother be enslaved. When Joseph saw that, maybe he felt there was some hope that the mess the brothers had made of their relationship could change, too, and he revealed his true identity to his brothers, and they all began to repair the broken parts of their relationships.

After telling the story, divide into groups. Each group will have one scene to pose for, like a snapshot of that scene, and everyone else will try to guess what part of the story it is. Then discuss how different people in the story might have been feeling during that scene.
Scenes:
- Joseph bragging about his brothers bowing down and being his father's favorite
- Joseph in the well; Reuben trying to stop them from killing them; the brothers when telling their father "what happened"
- Joseph in Egypt when he recognized his brothers, who were bowing down to him and trying to buy grain
- Joseph and his brothers when Joseph accused them of wrongdoing
- Joseph and his brothers when Joseph reveals who he is
- Alternatively, rather than having the groups decide for themselves how they will pose for the scene, another way to handle this is that you as the leader can also ask for volunteers for each scene, and pose them yourself, helping them wonder about how they would be feeling as you go.

"Wondering" Questions:
Throughout the posing for the scenes, ask questions like:

- I wonder how Joseph was feeling right then? I wonder how his brothers were feeling right then? I wonder how their father was feeling or would have been feeling right then? I wonder what Joseph was hoping for (revenge?) To try to get back at them and be mean to them as they were mean to him? A test to see if they had repented/changed/were sorry?

Or reconciliation… to try to have his family back together again? I wonder why Joseph tried to trick them? I wonder if Joseph wanted his brothers to feel sorry? I wonder if his brothers did feel sorry? I wonder why Joseph still revealed himself to his brothers and took good care of them even though they never said they were sorry?

Summary Statement (summarize main idea & connect back to theme):
Joseph and his brothers got in a mess, and little messes led to bigger ones. It started when Joseph was his father's favorite, and also when he was kind of arrogant and braggy. That hurt his brothers. So, they wanted to hurt Joseph. They didn't kill him, but they did hurt him and get rid of him. They set him up for a life of misery. God took care of Joseph, though, and he was in charge of selling food in Egypt. When Joseph's brothers came to buy grain, he could have hurt them back and not let them buy any and let them starve.

He tested them to see if they could be trusted, to see if they had changed at all. He set up a situation where they could endanger their father's other favorite son, Benjamin, just like they had endangered Joseph. But Judah, the one who sold Joseph into slavery, was willing to put himself in slavery instead. It seemed like Judah had grown and was sorry and was willing to repair things even when it would cost him. So, it seems Joseph wanted to have a relationship with them, but he needed to know if it was safe and if they had changed. In the end, though, he took care of them.

Sometimes we are like Joseph, and people have wronged us, and we have the opportunity to hurt them back or to take care of them. Sometimes we are like Joseph's brothers, and we have been mean to others, and we have to figure out a way to admit it and to try to make it right.

Either way, sometimes we get in a mess, where we've hurt people or been hurt, and we might be angry or sad. When we get in that kind of mess, when our friendships and relationships are in a mess, we have to have courage to face it, so we can try to fix it.

LEADER TIP: We want to be careful that we are not asking children to reenact slavery or things that might be traumatic for them. We are simply pausing at points in the story to wonder about how the characters might be feeling in that moment. A good practice to is let the children lead in giving ideas about how characters might be feeling and not try to manufacture feelings or try to get them to feel a certain way.

LEADER TIP: This story is not about forgiving those who have caused you damage without conditions or consequences. It seems Joseph's tests were designed to see if his brothers could be trusted, if they had changed, if they were willing to repair the damage (or prevent damage in Benjamin's case), even if it cost them something. When Judah was willing to be sold into slavery to spare Benjamin, Joseph knew he had changed. That's when the relationship could be worked on. We can forgive without reconciling. But reconciliation takes repentance and repairing damage.

Story Book 2

There are several options for this storybook time. As mentioned, when humans see difference, they often respond by letting it separate them, or even by using it as an excuse to treat those they see as different as less than they are. The first two books are examples of how something (fear) holds us back from good relationships, and how we have to be brave to reach out and build friendships with others, to not let our differences or fear separate us, but to come together, which is God's dream for us. The other books are all examples of how human beings encountered differences, and instead of living into God's dream and being blessed by the beauty in diversity, instead of seeing the image of God in each person, humans instead reacted with fear, anger, and violence, treating those who they perceived as different as inferior; that did damage and made a mess of our relationships, keeping us separated from one another.

Examples include:

- *I Am Not A Number* about Native Americans, and trying to erase their differences through residential schools
- *Henry's Freedom Box* about enslaving people from Africa, and treating them as less than human
- *Ruth and the Green Book* about segregation, and still treating people of color as inferior
- *Barbed Wire Baseball* about Japanese American internment camps, treating anyone who was Japanese with fear and suspicion, unfairly imprisoning them
- Please note that Latinx references are coming in Lesson 3.

It is important for children to learn the ways we have messed up God's dream, the ways we refuse to see God's image in others, the way we don't see diversity as beautiful. When this happens, it makes a mess. Some of these stories are difficult, but it is important for children to hear them. Children can be brave to face these messes and to help work on them. They also can be brave not to repeat these things, and instead to learn how to see diversity as a blessing, something that shows us more of what God is like.

In this section, you might want to choose several examples of how human beings have messed up God's dream, either by letting difference separate us instead of bringing us together, or by treating others as "less than" instead of honoring and being blessed by the beauty their uniqueness brings.

Remind them when we hear stories where humans messed things up, that we can be brave to face these things, so that we can help work to make the world as God intended it to be.

LEADER TIP: In choosing storybooks, we've used resources to help evaluate them and their messaging. Miriam McKenney curates a list of resources, and as someone doing the work of dismantling racism and formation work in the church, provides unique insight in what she recommends. You can find her recommendations on the Building Faith website in an article called "Picture Books for Anti-Racists."

Also, Social Justice Books provide great reviews for most of the books on the lists on their website, including what caveats they might add to enhance the discussion. https://socialjusticebooks.org/

Brave Molly (Pre-K/K)

Overview for Leader:
Brave Molly, by Brooke Boynton Hughes, is a unique book. It is a book of illustrations, no words. However, the pictures tell the story of Molly's fears and what she does to overcome those fears. The story can be told interactively with the leader helping the children tell Molly's story. It's a story that helps children learn that being brave can be scary, but the more we try, the less scary it is.

Repeated Ideas for Lesson 2 "I Am Brave":
- God's Dream: God made us all different, and that is beautiful! God intended differences to bless us and enrich us. We need each other to see God (like the puzzle), and we need each other to be whole, full humans (like how we're all like different parts of a Team).
- The mess: Humans have often looked down on differences and responded by either (1) letting differences separate us or (2) treating those who are different with unfairness. When we let differences separate us instead of bringing us together, when we treat other humans with unfairness, we mess up God's dream. We make a mess.
- Being Brave: When we see that differences have separated us, we must be brave to reach out and invite others to come together as God intended. When we see that there is a mess (hurt, people being left out, unfairness), we must be brave to face the messes and try to work on them and fix them.
- With God's help, we can help make the messes into something beautiful.

Introductory Statement: In our Bible story we learned about Joseph and his brothers. Joseph's brothers did not want Joseph to have all the attention; it made them upset. So, they sent him away. Once Joseph's brothers sent him away, Joseph was all alone. He went to a strange land. He did not have his family, and he did not have any friends. Being alone can be very scary. When you are alone, your feelings can feel like big scary voices coming after you. Joseph had to be brave. Instead of listening to those scary voices, he listened to God's voice and was able to find new friends, and the strange land became his home. In our story, Molly has to be brave. The voices that are screaming at Molly feel like monsters following her around, and she has to find her brave voice.

Read the Story: *Brave Molly* by Brooke Boynton-Hughes, Chronicle Publishing, 2019. If you have a copy, you can read it, or you can show a video of someone reading it. There are several options on YouTube to choose from. It is a story with no words, so the reader creates the story. If you have a copy, you can invite the children to help in telling the story.

"Wondering" Questions:
- I wonder if you have ever been afraid? What were you afraid of?
- I wonder if there was someone who helped you be brave? What did they tell you?
- I wonder how you can help someone else feel brave? Can you be brave and scared at the same time?

Summary Statement (summarize main idea of story & connect back to theme):
When we feel alone or afraid, it is hard to be brave. There are distractions all around us telling us that we should stay afraid. We have to listen, closely, for the voice of God. God will let us know what we need to do to be brave.

Have someone read Psalm 23 or read together as a group.

The Lion Inside (Pre-K/K)

Overview for Leader:
The Lion Inside, by Rachel Bright and Jim Field, is a sweet story about a mouse that seeks out the brave lion so that it can learn how to make a brave roar and be noticed. But when the mouse meets the lion, it learns that even lions have things they are afraid of. It's a story that helps children learn that you can be both scared and brave at the same time.

Repeated Ideas for Lesson 2 "I Am Brave":
- God's Dream: God made us all different, and that is beautiful! God intended differences to bless us and enrich us. We need each other to see God (like the puzzle), and we need each other to be whole, full humans (like how we're all like different parts of a Team).
- The mess: Humans have often looked down on differences and responded by either (1) letting differences separate us or (2) treating those who are different with unfairness. When we let differences separate us instead of bringing us together, when we treat other humans with unfairness, we mess up God's dream. We make a mess.
- Being Brave: When we see that differences have separated us, we must be brave to reach out and invite others to come together as God intended. When we see that there is a mess (hurt, people being left out, unfairness), we must be brave to face the messes and try to work on them and fix them.
- With God's help, we can help make the messes into something beautiful.

Introductory Statement:
Today we are talking about how sometimes we create messes and that we show love for God by cleaning them up. Some of our messes are really big, and it can be hard to figure out how to fix such a big mess. It takes a lot of bravery to start the work of cleaning up a big mess. But no matter who you are or how big you are, you can be brave and help with the work. This story is about a mouse that discovers how to be brave.

Read the Story: *The Lion Inside* by Rachel Bright and illustrated by Jim Field, Orchard Books, 2016

"Wondering" Questions:
- I wonder if you have ever felt like you were too small to be noticed. When do you feel that way? What do people do around you that make you feel like you aren't noticed?
- I wonder if you know anyone who is always noticed. Why do you notice that person?

- I wonder if you ever met an adult who was afraid of something. What were they afraid of? Were you also afraid of that thing, or was it something that doesn't scare you?
- I wonder if it's possible to be brave and scared at the same time.
- I wonder if there has ever been a time when you were scared and brave at the same time.

Summary Statement (summarize main idea of story & connect back to theme):
Sometimes when we are young, it can feel impossible to be brave like older kids or adults. They seem to really have it all together! But the truth is, even grown-ups have things that they are afraid of; they have just had more practice at being brave and facing their fears. God has asked all of us, no matter how young or small we are, to be brave and speak up when we see things that make God sad. In fact, sometimes children are even better at seeing the things that make God sad, so they are even better equipped to help! No matter where you are, you can always be looking out for ways to fix things that make God sad, even if it means you have to be brave.

I Am Not a Number (upper elementary, about colonialism)

Overview for Leader:
This is one example of the ways that human beings saw differences as a bad thing, and then treated those who they perceived as different unjustly. We have done that throughout our history in the United States, even before there was a United States. This book talks about the ways the government and those in power tried to erase differences in Native Americans' culture and language by using violence through residential boarding schools.

Repeated Ideas for Lesson 2 "I Am Brave":
- God's Dream: God made us all different, and that is beautiful! God intended differences to bless us and enrich us. We need each other to see God (like the puzzle), and we need each other to be whole, full humans (like how we're all like different parts of a Team).
- The mess: Humans have often looked down on differences and responded by either (1) letting differences separate us or (2) treating those who are different with unfairness. When we let differences separate us instead of bringing us together, when we treat other humans with unfairness, we mess up God's dream. We make a mess.
- Being Brave: When we see that differences have separated us, we must be brave to reach out and invite others to come together as God intended. When we see that there is a mess (hurt, people being left out, unfairness), we must be brave to face the messes and try to work on them and fix them.
- With God's help, we can help make the messes into something beautiful.

Introductory Statement:
This story is about how when White people from Europe encountered the beautiful differences between them and Native American people, they tried to erase those differences, and force Native Americans to become like White people. God's dream is that we would see the image of God through our differences, that we would see the beauty that God created in each person. But humans instead often try to treat those with differences as inferior (less than). This is a story where human beings made a mess. If only we had followed God's dream and seen those differences, the Native Americans' unique culture and language and perspective, as a blessing! We need each other, and we need each other's differences and perspectives! But instead, White colonizers viewed it as bad and tried to take away those God-given differences. Humans made a mess. But remember, we can be brave to face those messes, so we can try to fix them.

Read the Story: *I Am Not a Number* by Dr. Jenny Kay Dupuis and Kathy Kacer, illustrated by Gillian Newland, Second Story Press, 2016

"Wondering" Questions:
- I wonder what it would be like if you or I were taken away from our parents when we were young, and we were made to learn a different language and culture?
- The author said that it was important to tell this story about her grandmother. I wonder why she thought it was so important?
- These residential schools caused many Native Americans to forget their language and lose their culture. I wonder how that problem might be faced? I wonder how that might be made right?

Summary Statement (summarize main idea of story & connect back to theme):
- Beauty in diversity: When faced with some beautiful differences they found in the Native Americans, White colonizers did what humans often do: they treated those who were different as less worthy than they were.
- We need each other: We need the perspectives and beauty of Native Americans' language and culture. Differences make us better and stronger.
- The mess: They tried to erase those differences, and it made a huge mess. Still today, we don't even know the extent of the damage this has caused. Some Native Americans lost their language. Some lost their families forever. Many died. It's still a mess. The United States is still working to find just how much of a mess is still left behind from these residential schools. To try to help fix that mess, we need to know about it.

LEADER TIP: Learn more about what the U.S. is doing to find out how much of a mess is still left behind by visiting the Department of the Interior government website and searching for a press release by Secretary of the Interior, Debbie Haaland, about the Federal Indian Boarding School Initiative. In response to Canada's finding 215 unmarked graves at one of their Indian Residential Schools, Secretary Haaland has directed that a report be made, detailing all historical records of U.S. federal boarding schools, especially on potential burial sites, and noting the intergenerational trauma and impact of the boarding schools in the U.S. She said "it won't undo the heartbreak and loss that we feel. But only by acknowledging the past can we work toward a future that we're all proud to embrace." More resources on this, and also on the Episcopal Church's response, can be found on the Diocese of Atlanta website under Resources (go to Education & Formation, then Dismantling Racism Curriculum Resources).

Henry's Freedom Box (elementary, about slavery)

Overview for Leader:
This story is about the true story of Henry Brown's ingenious escape from slavery to freedom. It talks about some of the experiences of those who were enslaved, and how they did not even have the freedom to be with their families, spouses, and children. It also depicts Henry as someone who endures with resilience, and through ingenuity and help from friends, escapes to freedom.

Repeated Ideas for Lesson 2 "I Am Brave":
- God's Dream: God made us all different, and that is beautiful! God intended differences to bless us and enrich us. We need each other to see God (like the puzzle), and we need each other to be whole, full humans (like how we're all like different parts of a Team).
- The mess: Humans have often looked down on differences and responded by either (1) letting differences separate us or (2) treating those who are different with unfairness. When we let differences separate us instead of bringing us together, when we treat other humans with unfairness, we mess up God's dream. We make a mess.
- Being Brave: When we see that differences have separated us, we must be brave to reach out and invite others to come together as God intended. When we see that there is a mess (hurt, people being left out, unfairness), we must be brave to face the messes and try to work on them and fix them.
- With God's help, we can help make the messes into something beautiful.

Introductory Statement:
This book is about the ways that we have made a mess. When some White humans encountered differences in culture and skin color, they took advantage of those differences and used them as an excuse to treat those with dark skin as less than human, to steal their labor and force them to make things better for White people. That's what slavery was in our country. This book helps us understand a little bit more about the experiences of the enslaved and the mess that was made when many White people denied the image of God in Africans and African Americans. Humans made a mess, but still there is hope that things can change, and we see some even in this book.

Read the Story: *Henry's Freedom Box: A True Story from the Underground Railroad* by Ellen Levine, illustrated by Kadir Nelson, Scholastic Press, 2007

"Wondering" Questions:
- I wonder what you felt when you learned how Henry and others who were enslaved were treated? I wonder how you felt when you saw Henry's plan to escape to freedom? I wonder where you saw some hope that things could get better in this book? I wonder where you saw kindness in this book?
- When humans started treating Black people unjustly, it was a long time ago, but the damage and hurt from that is still around today. Many of the Africans who were enslaved never were able to go back to their homes or families. Sometimes in this world, humans still treat others unjustly. I wonder how this problem might be faced? That is a hard problem to fix, but remember, we can be brave and face things that are hard, and with God's help, we can make beautiful things out of messes. I wonder how we can keep trying to work on this mess to make it better?

Summary Statement (summarize main idea of story & connect back to theme):
- Beauty in diversity: When faced with some beautiful differences they found in the African Americans, White colonizers did what humans often do: they treated those who were different as less worthy than they were, and in the case of slavery, as less than human.
- We need each other: We need the perspectives and beauty of people of color. Differences make us better and stronger.
- The mess: Slavery was a terrible, terrible injustice, where the differences God intended to be a blessing to humanity (like differences in culture and skin color) White people used to treat others as less than human and stole their labor. Humans made a mess. You and I didn't make that mess no matter what our skin color is, but it's still a mess, and it has caused hurt and pain for Black people; that hurt and pain is still with us today. Sometimes people with non-white skin are still treated unfairly, even today. It's a hard mess to clean up, but remember that we can be brave. We can face huge problems, because God is with us, and God can help us fix these big messes.

Ruth and the Green Book (elementary, about segregation)

Overview for Leader:
This book is based on the true history of the Green Book, which was a book people of color used during segregation to help them know the places, hotels, business, etc. that were welcoming to black people. It was an essential safety measure to take when traveling, as it was dangerous for people of color during segregation.

Repeated Ideas for Lesson 2 "I Am Brave":
- God's Dream: God made us all different, and that is beautiful! God intended differences to bless us and enrich us. We need each other to see God (like the puzzle), and we need each other to be whole, full humans (like how we're all like different parts of a Team).
- The mess: Humans have often looked down on differences and responded by either (1) letting differences separate us or (2) treating those who are different with unfairness. When we let differences separate us instead of bringing us together, when we treat other humans with unfairness, we mess up God's dream. We make a mess.
- Being Brave: When we see that differences have separated us, we must be brave to reach out and invite others to come together as God intended. When we see that there is a mess (hurt, people being left out, unfairness), we must be brave to face the messes and try to work on them and fix them.
- With God's help, we can help make the messes into something beautiful.

Introductory Statement:
This book is about the ways that we have made a mess. When White humans encountered differences in culture and skin color, they treated those with dark skin as less than human through slavery. Even after slavery ended, they still saw those beautiful differences as bad, and let them separate us all, instead of coming together and being made more complete as God intended. This story helps us understand a little bit more about segregation and the mess that was made when White people denied the image of God in African Americans and treated them as inferior and separate, leaving them out, through segregation.

Read the Story: *Ruth and the Green Book* by Calvin Alexander Ramsey and Gwen Strauss, illustrated by Floyd Cooper, Carolrhoda Books, 2010

"Wondering" Questions:
- I wonder if you've ever been on a road trip and spent the night in a hotel? I wonder if your family was ever denied a hotel room or a bathroom at a gas station because of the

color of your skin? I wonder what you felt when you heard the unfair treatment Ruth and her family went through? I wonder if there was anything in the story that gave you hope? I wonder if you saw kindness anywhere?
- Even though there are no more Jim Crow laws that force black people and white people to be segregated, human beings still have a tendency to exclude people. I wonder if you've ever been excluded and what that was like for you? I wonder if you've ever been invited and included, and what that was like? I wonder how we can make the world more of the kind of world that invites people to be included and invited in instead of excluded and left out?

Summary Statement (summarize main idea of story & connect back to theme):
- Beauty in diversity: God made all kinds of people with beautiful differences, and God intended that those differences would bless us and make us more whole and complete, not separate us. When faced with some beautiful differences they found in the African Americans, White people did what humans often do: they treated those who were different as less worthy than they were, and in the case of segregation, allowed those differences to keep us apart rather than bringing us together.
- The mess: Segregation was a way to continue the injustices against people of color, even after slavery had ended. But humans, and in this case, white skinned human beings, looked at those differences and tried to separate people based on those differences. They treated people who were different from them, who had a different skin color, as less than they were, and they left them out and kept them separate, and it caused a lot of damage and hurt and pain. We read about the ways it really hurt Ruth's feelings and made her angry and sad. Excluding others is not God's dream for us.
- We need each other: When we include people and get to know those who are different from us, we are blessed! We become more fully human. And we see more of who God is. So, part of bringing God's dream to this earth is including others, not excluding them or leaving them out.

Barbed Wire Baseball (upper elementary, about Japanese internment)

Overview for Leader:
This story is about Japanese internment camps, another instance of White human beings who had power in our country viewing differences as dangerous, and using it as an excuse to treat others unfairly. This story gives insight about the experiences of those who were sent to internment camps and also the resiliency of those who were wrongfully imprisoned, and how they still found hope and a sense of home... through baseball.

Repeated Ideas for Lesson 2 "I Am Brave":
- God's Dream: God made us all different, and that is beautiful! God intended differences to bless us and enrich us. We need each other to see God (like the puzzle), and we need each other to be whole, full humans (like how we're all like different parts of a Team).
- The mess: Humans have often looked down on differences and responded by either (1) letting differences separate us or (2) treating those who are different with unfairness. When we let differences separate us instead of bringing us together, when we treat other humans with unfairness, we mess up God's dream. We make a mess.
- Being Brave: When we see that differences have separated us, we must be brave to reach out and invite others to come together as God intended. When we see that there is a mess (hurt, people being left out, unfairness), we must be brave to face the messes and try to work on them and fix them.
- With God's help, we can help make the messes into something beautiful.

Introductory Statement:
This book is about the ways that we have made a mess. When Japanese people emigrated to America, they were often mistreated because they were different from White European immigrants, but they made lives for themselves. When Pearl Harbor was bombed by the Japanese during World War II, the United States government viewed Japanese Americans with fear and suspicion. As humans often do, they viewed differences as dangerous or bad and wanted to use differences as an excuse to separate Japanese Americans, and they treated Japanese Americans badly. They took them from their homes and possessions, and unjustly put them in camps. This is the story of one Japanese American who brought hope to an internment camp during World War II.

Read the Story: *Barbed Wire Baseball: How One Man Brought Hope to the Japanese Internment Camps of WWII* by Marissa Moss, illustrated by Yuko Shimizu, published by Harry N. Abrams, 2013

"Wondering" Questions:
- I wonder where you see unfairness and unkindness in the story?
- I wonder what you thought of the Japanese Americans being imprisoned just because of what the Japanese in another country did?
- I wonder where you saw hope and happiness in the story?
- Baseball was something familiar, that felt like home while they were in the internment camp. I wonder what are things, like a shared love of sports or baseball, that can help bring different people together and make them feel at home? They might be things that all humans like… I wonder what are the things that people around the world share or have in common *(possible answers: playing, sports, music, family, eating, wanting safety, loving their families)*?
- I wonder how we can use those shared things to bring people together instead of separating us?

Summary Statement (summarize main idea of story & connect back to theme):
- Beauty in Diversity: God gave us the gift of diversity, of people looking different and having different personalities and abilities, so we could see more of what God is like, and so we could be blessed and be more complete, because we need each other.
- The mess: Human beings have often seen those differences with fear or suspicion and have used differences to separate and exclude others. This story is one example of how humans have done that. They were so afraid, they separated Japanese people into these camps and excluded them.
- We need each other: The story is also a reminder that there are things we all hold in common, that draw us together and make us feel at home, even when we might have differences. That's one way we can fix the mess we've made by trying to separate from each other… we can find out things we have in common, and we can share experiences together.

Personal Story 2 | Stories of Seeing Difference & Facing Messes

Overview for Leader: There are two options for today's personal story on one of these themes: (1) being brave to face a mess you made (a literal mess, or a relational mess), and/or (2) the story of learning to see differences differently…of moving from being afraid of differences to valuing the beauty of every person God has created.

Repeated Ideas for Lesson 2 "I Am Brave":
- God's Dream: God made us all different, and that is beautiful! God intended differences to bless us and enrich us. We need each other to see God (like the puzzle), and we need each other to be whole, full humans (like how we're all like different parts of a Team).
- The mess: Humans have often looked down on differences and responded by either (1) letting differences separate us or (2) treating those who are different with unfairness. When we let differences separate us instead of bringing us together, when we treat other humans with unfairness, we mess up God's dream. We make a mess.
- Being Brave: When we see that differences have separated us, we must be brave to reach out and invite others to come together as God intended. When we see that there is a mess (hurt, people being left out, unfairness), we must be brave to face the messes and try to work on them and fix them.
- With God's help, we can help make the messes into something beautiful.

Story Option 1: Being Brave to Face a Mess

Introductory Statement: Sometimes, we hurt people or make mistakes, and it makes a mess. It could be accidentally breaking something, or it could be saying mean, hurtful words. We all mess things up sometimes. When we do, we have to be brave to face it and to try to make it right.

Share the Story:
(Use your own or use one from the authors. You can also visit the Diocese of Atlanta website under Resources>Education & Formation, and click on the section for Dismantling Racism curriculum to see more video stories there)

Story Example: I remember one time I was driving my uncle's truck through a rugged trail in the woods, and I bumped a tree. I was so scared to tell him about it. But I knew that if I wanted to fix the mess, I had to be brave, and I had to talk to him. (He was very gracious and not concerned). When we mess up, we have to be brave to face it. We can't run away and leave a mess. We have to face it and try to fix it, and that takes so much courage! It would probably be easier to run away from the mess we've made, but it doesn't help anything! We need to be brave in order to face the messes humans have made by being so mean to each other, so that we can try to help fix it. —Sally Ulrey

Summary Statement (summarize main idea of story & connect back to theme):
When we make a mess, we have to be brave to face that mess and not hide from it. It takes courage, but nothing will get better until we face it! Not everything gets fixed so easily, but we have to try to do what we can.

Story Option 2: Stories of Seeing Differences

Introductory Statement: God made every single human being on this planet special and unique. There is no one like you. Everyone is different. That's so cool! Every time we come across a difference, we can learn something. Those who are different from us have unique experiences and perspectives that can be a gift. But we don't always see it like that. Sometimes we see differences, and we make fun of those who are different. Sometimes we see differences, and we are mean to those who are different. Sometimes we see differences, and we leave out those who are different. Sometimes we are afraid. When we treat people who are different from us with unkindness, that is not what God intended, and we mess things up when we do that. We mess up our friendships. And we miss out on the blessing of knowing all those unique people who are all made in the image of God, so we miss out on learning more about what God is like! But we can LEARN to see differences in a new way. We can learn to see those who are different from us as God intended, as beautiful and amazing and beloved, and their perspective can be a beautiful gift!

Share a Story: Share a story of a time you initially encountered a difference (and we are specifically speaking of racial, ethnic, and cultural differences in this conversation), and you initially (perhaps even unconsciously at first) reacted with fear, suspicion, or distancing. Share how you learned to view these differences in a new way, and how seeing things from a new perspective was a blessing that helped you be more fully human and complete.

Summary Statement: (summarize main idea of story & connect back to theme):
We sometimes are afraid of differences and treat those with differences poorly. That makes a mess of relationships, but we can learn to do things differently. We can learn to see differences as God intended: as beautiful, as a blessing. We can remember that we need each other, everyone, that we need all the different perspectives and abilities and gifts. That's the good news! We can learn how to do better!

Art 2 | Beauty Out of the Mess

Option 1: Mosaic (Pottery or Paper)

Supplies:
Tiles of all different colors
Hammer
Modge Podge, or some other type of glue that can be brushed on
Flat wood or ceramic surface to put mosaic on, about the size of a Christmas ornament. You can find these in craft stores.

OR

Tissue paper of all different colors
Glue
"Ornament-sized" surface for paper to go on (or a sheet of construction paper)

Overview for Leader:
This activity focuses on the hope we have as Christians that God can make something beautiful out of all the messes we make, out of all the ways we mess up God's dream and intention for us. Things are never too far gone that we can't hold on to the truth that God can do anything, even make something beautiful out of a big, broken mess. This is an analogy/illustration, so especially with younger children, build careful and intentional bridges from the concrete "mess" of the torn tissue paper or smashed tile to the abstract "mess" of when we break our relationships by being mean and unfair. You will have to be really clear in your language here.

Repeated Ideas for Lesson 2 "I Am Brave":
- God's Dream: God made us all different, and that is beautiful! God intended differences to bless us and enrich us. We need each other to see God (like the puzzle), and we need each other to be whole, full humans (like how we're all like different parts of a Team).
- The mess: Humans have often looked down on differences and responded by either (1) letting differences separate us or (2) treating those who are different with unfairness. When we let differences separate us instead of bringing us together, when we treat other humans with unfairness, we mess up God's dream. We make a mess.
- Being Brave: When we see that differences have separated us, we must be brave to reach out and invite others to come together as God intended. When we see that there is a mess

(hurt, people being left out, unfairness), we must be brave to face the messes and try to work on them and fix them.
- With God's help, we can help make the messes into something beautiful.

Introductory Statement: Sometimes we make a mess of things. Humans hurt people, and when they see others are different, they are mean to them, instead of celebrating them as God's beloved child. And when humans are mean to each other, it breaks things, and it makes a mess. But if we're brave enough, we can face that mess, and start to work on it. And when we do, God helps us to make something beautiful out of it. But we have to face the mess. We can't leave it like that, even if that would be easier. We have to clean it up and keep working on it, until we can make it beautiful with God's help.

Instructions:
- Remind children of some of the ways we've made a mess and hurt people (slavery, segregation, treating others as "less than").
- Each time we remember something from history where humans hurt each other, smash a tile (rip a paper). Talk about how in doing that unfair and hurtful thing, we have broken our relationships with one another. We might think, what good can ever come out of this? But God can do anything!
- Then instruct them on how to make a beautiful mosaic out of the broken, messed up pieces.

Summary Statement (summarize main idea of art & connect back to the theme):
- Differences are beautiful, and they show us something about God. Sometimes, humans see differences, and instead of seeing the beauty and the blessings, they see differences as bad, and use it as a reason to be mean and unkind.
- Humans mess up God's beautiful dream for the world when we hurt each other and treat each other badly. We make a mess. We've done it MANY times.
- When we see a mess, God wants us to face it, and to work on it, and to try to help God make it into something beautiful.
- We have to be brave and face the messes and the problems. God is with us!
- Humans have not finished making beauty out of messes yet (it will take a long time and lots of work), but this artwork you've made today can remind us to keep trying.

Option 2: Bravery Medals

Supplies:
Cardboard or thick cardstock
Cookie cutters or stencils (in star or other medallion shapes)
Scissors
Paint and brushes
Glue
Sequins, glitter, stickers, etc.
About 1" wide ribbon
Safety pins

Overview for Leader: In this activity, younger children will have a chance to celebrate the ways they have been brave in both big and small ways. We don't often spend a lot of time celebrating the smaller ways that kids need to be brave, like inviting a new friend to play with them or disagreeing with their friends when they have done or said something unkind. In this activity, the children will get the chance to do so!

Repeated Ideas for Lesson 2 "I Am Brave":
- God's Dream: God made us all different, and that is beautiful! God intended differences to bless us and enrich us. We need each other to see God (like the puzzle), and we need each other to be whole, full humans (like how we're all like different parts of a Team).
- The mess: Humans have often looked down on differences and responded by either (1) letting differences separate us or (2) treating those who are different with unfairness. When we let differences separate us instead of bringing us together, when we treat other humans with unfairness, we mess up God's dream. We make a mess.
- Being Brave: When we see that differences have separated us, we must be brave to reach out and invite others to come together as God intended. When we see that there is a mess (hurt, people being left out, unfairness), we must be brave to face the messes and try to work on them and fix them.
- With God's help, we can help make the messes into something beautiful.

Introductory Statement:
Throughout our lives, we will be growing and learning. A lot of times that is fun and carefree, but other times we have to be brave and do or say something we have never done before. We may even have to do or say something that we think others would disagree with, like standing up for someone who is not being treated well or inviting a new kid to play with you on the playground. It takes bravery to choose to do something that is unexpected or comes with a

risk, and all of those things add up to help fix some of the messes that we have made in this world. In this activity, we are going to spend some time celebrating those small acts of bravery that are making this world a better reflection of God's dream.

Instructions:

- Spend some time talking with the children about all the different ways we are required to be brave to show that we love God, even as children. Give them examples and allow them to share their experiences.
- Invite them to create a bravery medal to celebrate one of the times that they were brave.
- Use the cookie cutters of templates to trace and cut out medallion shapes from the cardboard/cardstock. Depending on time constraints and the age of the children, this is something you may want to prep beforehand.
- Paint the medallions.
- Once dry, decorate the medallions with sequin, glitter, stickers, or any other fun item you can dig up.
- Attach a strip 3"-4" of ribbon on the back of the medallion with glue or tape.
- Allow the children to share what their bravery medals represent, and then use the safety pins to affix the medal to the child.
- Encourage them to wear their medals home and share with their adults about their bravery!

Summary Statement (summarize main idea of art & connect back to the theme): God has called us to help create a world where we treat everyone fairly, but a lot of times we mess that up. If we want to help fix that mess, we will likely have to say and do many brave things, both big and small. These medals are a reminder of that work that God has invited us to do. Some of us can remember doing brave things that are big, and others can remember doing many small acts. God knows and sees all of them and us whenever we choose to do something brave that helps others know and love God better.

Craft inspired by: laughingkidslearn.com

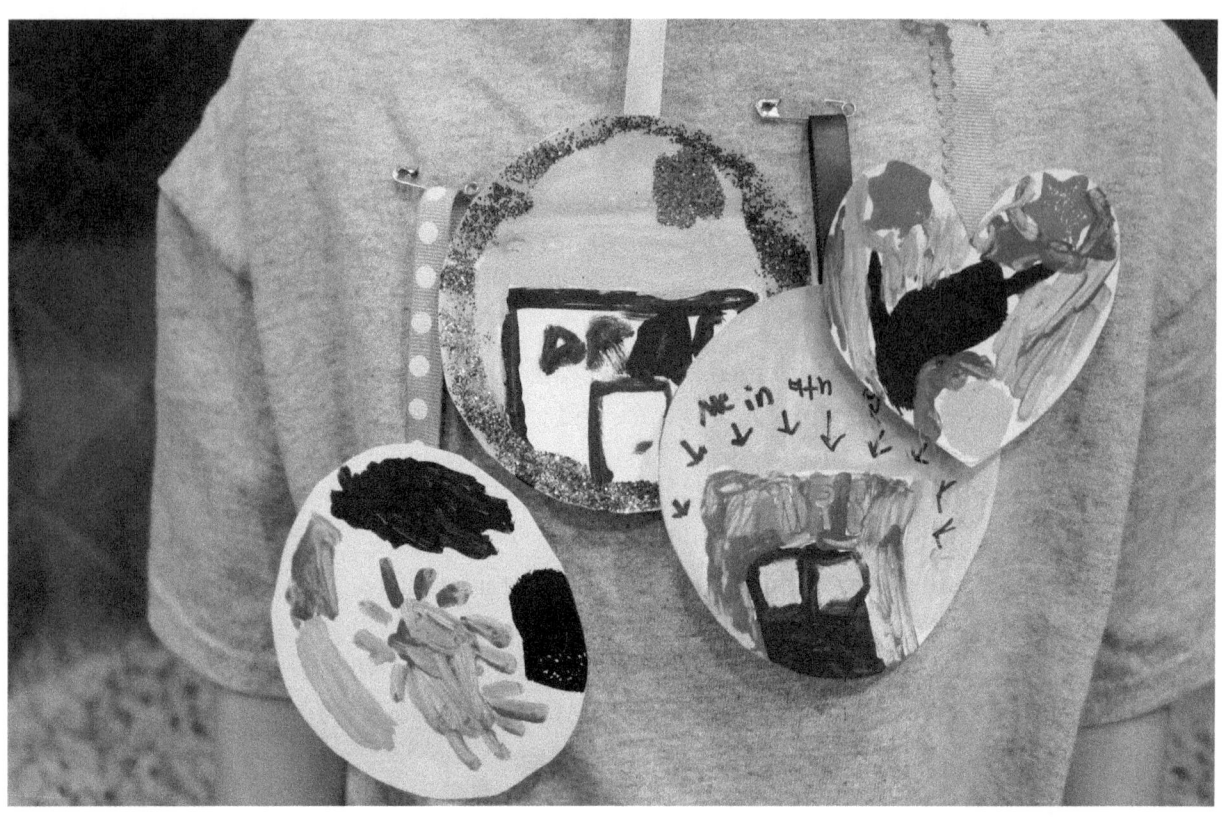

Music 2

Songs: "Brave," "Brave Enough," "Beautiful Things"

<u>Song #1</u>: "Brave" by David Dalton, John Cassetto, Jyro LaVilla, Socrates Perez, Stefanie Cassetto, Temree Miller. Label: InResponse Music, 2014. This song is covered by CCLI.

Overview for Leader:
This song is about how God is always with us and always loves us, no matter what we face. Knowing that, we can be brave. God loves us no matter what, and when we rest in that, we can be brave to face hard things, or even to face it when we make mistakes, because we will always, always be loved by God.

Repeated Ideas for Lesson 2 "I Am Brave":
- God's Dream: God made us all different, and that is beautiful! God intended differences to bless us and enrich us. We need each other to see God (like the puzzle), and we need each other to be whole, full humans (like how we're all like different parts of a Team).
- The mess: Humans have often looked down on differences and responded by either (1) letting differences separate us or (2) treating those who are different with unfairness. When we let differences separate us instead of bringing us together, when we treat other humans with unfairness, we mess up God's dream. We make a mess.
- Being Brave: When we see that differences have separated us, we must be brave to reach out and invite others to come together as God intended. When we see that there is a mess (hurt, people being left out, unfairness), we must be brave to face the messes and try to work on them and fix them.
- With God's help, we can help make the messes into something beautiful.

Introductory Statement to Singing the Song: There are times when we need to be brave, because we have to face the things that we might otherwise avoid. If we really want to help fix the world, we have to face the messes in it. But we CAN be brave, and we CAN face those messes, even messes we've helped create; even when we mess up, we can face it and try to fix it because we know that no matter what, we are LOVED by God. When we know that we are loved, even if we mess up, even when we're afraid, and there is nothing we could ever do to lose that love, it makes us brave. We can face things and fix messes. We can apologize if we need to and be kind to others even when we're afraid they might reject us, because you know who will never reject us? God! We will always be loved by God no matter what. And when we know that we will always be loved, and we can never lose that love, we can be brave. God's love makes us brave to face whatever we need to face and fix whatever mess we need to fix.

Special Instructions/Motions: This song already has choreographed movements that you can search for online if you want to use them.

Summary Statement (summarize main idea & connect back to the theme):
That song is about how God will always love us no matter what. There is nothing we can do that would make God love us less, and God already loves us as much as ever. And when we know we are loved no matter what, we can be brave. We can be brave to face big messes and fix them. We can be brave to apologize to someone if needed. We can be brave to reach out to someone in kindness, even if we're afraid they might be unkind back. Because no matter whether other people like us or not, we are loved. God always loves us, and that makes us brave.

<u>Song #2</u>: "Brave Enough" by Amanda Meisenheimer. Songsheets and licenses for this song can be purchased from Illustrated Ministry.

Overview for Leader:
This song is about how we CAN be brave to love, to listen, and to hear hard truths that we might otherwise want to avoid. But we are brave!

Repeated Ideas for Lesson 2 "I Am Brave":
- God's Dream: God made us all different, and that is beautiful! God intended differences to bless us and enrich us. We need each other to see God (like the puzzle), and we need each other to be whole, full humans (like how we're all like different parts of a Team).
- The mess: Humans have often looked down on differences and responded by either (1) letting differences separate us or (2) treating those who are different with unfairness. When we let differences separate us instead of bringing us together, when we treat other humans with unfairness, we mess up God's dream. We make a mess.
- Being Brave: When we see that differences have separated us, we must be brave to reach out and invite others to come together as God intended. When we see that there is a mess (hurt, people being left out, unfairness), we must be brave to face the messes and try to work on them and fix them.
- With God's help, we can help make the messes into something beautiful.

Introductory Statement to Singing the Song: This song talks about some of the things we can do because we're brave. We can love, we can show compassion, we can listen, we can tell the truth. I wonder if you can think of some ways we can love each other right now? I wonder if you can think of some ways that we can show compassion right now? I wonder if we can think of ways we can listen to each other? I wonder if we can think of ways we could tell the truth?

Special Instructions/Motions: From their brainstorming session above, you might get ideas about what motions they can do during the song. For example, if they show love by giving an arm around the shoulder, a brief hug, or a high five, they could do that during that part of the song. If they can show compassion by helping someone up, they could act that out, by one person sitting on the floor and another helping them stand during that part.

Summary Statement (summarize main idea & connect back to the theme):
Because God loves us, we can be brave. Some ways we can be brave are to love each other, to reach out and help each other, to notice when someone is left out and invite them to be included. We can face things that are hard. We can listen to the hard truth that sometimes humans mess things up. We can be brave to face big messes that seem impossible, because we know that God makes beautiful things out of messes!

<u>**Song #3**</u>: "Beautiful Things" by Michael and Lisa Gungor, 2010. This is covered by CCLI (song #5665521).

Overview for Leader:
This song is about how God can make beautiful things out of anything, including us! When we partner with God, we can help God make something beautiful out of every mess. And God is making something beautiful out of us, too!

Repeated Ideas for Lesson 2 "I Am Brave":
- God's Dream: God made us all different, and that is beautiful! God intended differences to bless us and enrich us. We need each other to see God (like the puzzle), and we need each other to be whole, full humans (like how we're all like different parts of a Team).
- The mess: Humans have often looked down on differences and responded by either (1) letting differences separate us or (2) treating those who are different with unfairness. When we let differences separate us instead of bringing us together, when we treat other humans with unfairness, we mess up God's dream. We make a mess.
- Being Brave: When we see that differences have separated us, we must be brave to reach out and invite others to come together as God intended. When we see that there is a mess (hurt, people being left out, unfairness), we must be brave to face the messes and try to work on them and fix them.
- With God's help, we can help make the messes into something beautiful.

Introductory Statement to Singing the Song:
We've talked about how sometimes human beings see differences and treat those who are different as "less than" them. That makes a huge painful, broken mess. That is not what God intended. That was not God's dream for us. We sometimes mess things up, but God is so amazing that God can make something beautiful out of those painful messes. No mess is too big or too painful that God can't make something beautiful out of it. And God invites US to be a part of fixing those messes and making them into something beautiful. So this song is a reminder that we can help make all the things that are messed up in this world, all the painful times people have been mean to each other and hurt each other...all those can be made beautiful with God's help.

Special Instructions/Motions:
This song has been choreographed before, so you can search online for ideas or have the children help you create some motions.

Summary Statement (summarize main idea & connect back to the theme):
Even when we feel like the messes are too big, and it would take so much to really work on them, nothing is impossible for God. God can bring something beautiful out of the biggest mess! And God invites us to help make something beautiful. God loves us and we can never lose that love, so we can be brave to face the messes that are made when humans are mean and treat each other badly; with God's help, we can make them into something beautiful again. It might be hard, but we can do it!

Play/Activity 2 | Bravery Scale

Option 1

Supplies: Chairs or Mats, Stickers that represent accomplishment

Overview for Leader:
This game will help reinforce what bravery looks like in everyday life, by contrasting the messes we make with the ways we can be brave when we or someone else is being treated unfairly. Often times we think of bravery as being a big thing that only grownups or superheroes do.

Repeated Ideas for Lesson 2 "I Am Brave":
- God's Dream: God made us all different, and that is beautiful! God intended differences to bless us and enrich us. We need each other to see God (like the puzzle), and we need each other to be whole, full humans (like how we're all like different parts of a Team).
- The mess: Humans have often looked down on differences and responded by either (1) letting differences separate us or (2) treating those who are different with unfairness. When we let differences separate us instead of bringing us together, when we treat other humans with unfairness, we mess up God's dream. We make a mess.
- Being Brave: When we see that differences have separated us, we must be brave to reach out and invite others to come together as God intended. When we see that there is a mess (hurt, people being left out, unfairness), we must be brave to face the messes and try to work on them and fix them.
- With God's help, we can help make the messes into something beautiful.

Introductory Statement: Being brave sometimes means going against our brother, sister, or friends and doing the right thing. When we do the right thing, people may laugh or get mad at us. When we choose to be brave, we can feel proud knowing that the right thing pleases God, and our parents will be proud too.

Instructions: Have the children stand. Name some things that everyone has done that were not right. Ex: Yelled at a sibling, broke a rule at home or school. Additionally, name things that show bravery. When they hear something that is brave, have them sit down. When they hear things that are not brave remain standing.

Debrief/Discussion:
I wonder if there were things we named that you related to? I wonder who has had a time when they did something that wasn't right? I wonder who has had a time when they did something that was brave? I wonder what it felt like to be doing something brave?

Option 2

Supplies: Stickers that represent accomplishment, like award stickers or trophy stickers

Overview for Leader:
Like option 1 this game will help reinforce what bravery looks like in everyday life by contrasting the messes we make with the ways we can be brave when we or someone else is being treated unfairly. Often times we think of bravery as being a big thing that only grownups or superheroes do. This option would be appropriate for younger children.

Repeated Ideas for Lesson 2 "I Am Brave":
- God's Dream: God made us all different, and that is beautiful! God intended differences to bless us and enrich us. We need each other to see God (like the puzzle), and we need each other to be whole, full humans (like how we're all like different parts of a Team).
- The mess: Humans have often looked down on differences and responded by either (1) letting differences separate us or (2) treating those who are different with unfairness. When we let differences separate us instead of bringing us together, when we treat other humans with unfairness, we mess up God's dream. We make a mess.
- Being Brave: When we see that differences have separated us, we must be brave to reach out and invite others to come together as God intended. When we see that there is a mess (hurt, people being left out, unfairness), we must be brave to face the messes and try to work on them and fix them.
- With God's help, we can help make the messes into something beautiful.

Introductory Statement: Being brave sometimes means going against our brother, sister, or friends and doing the right thing. When we do the right thing, people may laugh or get mad at us. When we choose to be brave, we can feel proud knowing that the right thing pleases God, and our parents will be proud too.

Instructions: Put children in groups of four. One person is Joseph, and one is Reuben. The other two are brothers. Have them act out the part of the story when Joseph's brothers are about to throw him in the well. Then, let them take turns being Reuben. Each of them should think of a brave thing they could say to their brothers when it is their turn to be Reuben so that Joseph is not thrown in the well.

Debrief/Discussion: Talk about why sometimes it is hard to be brave and do the right thing. Have everyone name one thing they will do to be brave and hand out stickers for participation.

Summary Statement (summarize main idea of activity & connect back to the theme): Reuben and his brothers were all upset with Joseph and wanted to get rid of him. However, Reuben did not think that was the right thing to do. Sometimes being brave means going against the crowd. Refusing to go along with siblings or friends can be a sign of bravery.

Snack 2 | Joseph in the Well

Supplies:
- Clear plastic cups (9 oz)
- Blue jello
- Sour Patch Kids

Overview for Leader: As the children eat their snack, they will be reminded that it's our job to help fix messes that we see… to help all the "Josephs" get out of their "wells," especially since they ended up there because of injustice. It's also important that we are never the reason someone ends up in a well in the first place. And if we are, it's especially important that we help get them out.

Repeated Ideas for Lesson 2 "I Am Brave":
- God's Dream: God made us all different, and that is beautiful! God intended differences to bless us and enrich us. We need each other to see God (like the puzzle), and we need each other to be whole, full humans (like how we're all like different parts of a Team).
- The mess: Humans have often looked down on differences and responded by either (1) letting differences separate us or (2) treating those who are different with unfairness. When we let differences separate us instead of bringing us together, when we treat other humans with unfairness, we mess up God's dream. We make a mess.
- Being Brave: When we see that differences have separated us, we must be brave to reach out and invite others to come together as God intended. When we see that there is a mess (hurt, people being left out, unfairness), we must be brave to face the messes and try to work on them and fix them.
- With God's help, we can help make the messes into something beautiful.

Introductory Statement:
When we treat other humans with unfairness, we mess up God's dream. We make a mess, like Joseph and his brothers made of their relationship. Whenever we see a mess, we must be brave to face the messes and try to work on them and fix them. With God's help, we can help make the messes into something beautiful. And we're actually going to remember those things while we eat our snack today!

Instructions:
- Summarize the Bible Story. Say something like, "Today's Bible story was about Joseph who was thrown into a well. His brothers were jealous of him and hurt that their father loved him the most, and so they wanted to get rid of him. So, they threw him in a well until they sold him into slavery."

- Summarize our themes. Say something like, "We know that God intended for human beings to see the beauty in each and every person. We know that sometimes we fail to do that, and we mess things up. We know that we need each other. We know that when things are messed up, we have to try to face that mess, and work on it and try to fix it."
- Tell them about the snack. Say something like, "Today you have a little person in this blue jello, which is like Joseph in the well. When we see someone in a well, we have to help get them out! When we see someone who needs help, we have to help! And we need to remember not to ever be the reason someone got into a well, too! Don't be the reason someone is hurt or left out! So, everyone, help get Joseph out of the well!"

Summary Statement (summarize main idea & connect back to the theme):
When you see someone in a well, you gotta help dig them out. That means that when we see something that's messed up or not right, when we see something that's unfair, we have to try to face it and make it right. And don't be part of the reason why that person got into the well. That means, don't be the one that treated someone else unfairly. We are brave, and we can do it!

Serve/Do 2 | "Be Brave By"

Supplies:
"List of Ways to Be Brave" worksheet, one per child

Overview for Leader: Serve/Do for Lesson Two is a little bit of a Choose Your Own Adventure! You will share several ways that children can be brave in their lives, and they will commit to completing at least one task on the before you meet again.

Repeated Ideas for Lesson 2 "I Am Brave":
- God's Dream: God made us all different, and that is beautiful! God intended differences to bless us and enrich us. We need each other to see God (like the puzzle), and we need each other to be whole, full humans (like how we're all like different parts of a Team).
- The mess: Humans have often looked down on differences and responded by either (1) letting differences separate us or (2) treating those who are different with unfairness. When we let differences separate us instead of bringing us together, when we treat other humans with unfairness, we mess up God's dream. We make a mess.
- Being Brave: When we see that differences have separated us, we must be brave to reach out and invite others to come together as God intended. When we see that there is a mess (hurt, people being left out, unfairness), we must be brave to face the messes and try to work on them and fix them.
- With God's help, we can help make the messes into something beautiful.

Introductory Statement:
We spent time today talking about how there are a lot of messes in this world, and we have been called by God to be brave and help clean up some of the mess. When we leave here today, we are going to challenge ourselves to do at least one thing to help clean up the mess before we come back together. We will pass out a "List of Ways to be Brave" that might give you some ideas, but you may have some good ones that aren't on the list. How will you be brave to fix the mess before we return?

Instructions:
- Remind the children about the themes of the day. Talk about how we sometimes make a mess, but we can also be brave enough to clean up that mess.
- Hand out the list of "Ways to Be Brave" worksheet and give them some time to look over it and decide on which items they would be willing to attempt during your time apart.

- Give them a chance to share what they plan to do, either with a friend or in the larger group.
- Close in prayer, asking for God to make each of us brave as we move into the world and find ways to fix the messes that we have all created.

Summary Statement (summarize main idea of activity & connect to the theme):
There is a lot to do to clean up the messes that we have all made, but no matter how old we are, we can help do the work of putting things back the way God intended. We can all find ways to be brave and set things right with our friends, family, and out in the world. God is with us in this work, and we have what it takes!

Ways to Be Brave!

1. Apologize to someone you have hurt. Ask if there is anything you can do to make it better.

2. Watch for people who need help. It may be a family member or someone you encounter while you are out with your family. Be brave and help them!

3. Is there a child at school, on the playground, or at one of your activities that is being left out? Invite them specifically to join you.

4. If you hear anyone speaking unkindly about another person, stop them. Tell them that you are not okay with what they are saying. If they won't stop, move away from them, and do not participate in the conversation.

5. Do you know of anyone that is struggling? Think about all the people you know: your family, friends, teachers, coaches, neighbors, church family, etc. It can include adults! Make them a card or other small treat to offer encouragement.

6. Keep a look out for the ways that those around you are special. Pay them a compliment, and let them know how they are special.

7. Read about advocacy groups, like the Native American Healing Coalition, that are working to clean up some of the messes in the world. Think about how they might inspire you to do some work of your own.

*This page is reproducible.

Resources 2

Please visit the Diocese of Atlanta Website (Go to Resources>Education & Formation Resources, and click on Dismantling Racism Curriculum Resources), for more resources on this history section. There is so much more to be learned about these topics and how to teach about them. At the Diocese of Atlanta's website, you'll find more resources to help leaders teach about Native Americans and the erasure of their culture, and the work that is going on toward healing, and how to support that work. There are also resources about how to teach about slavery and segregation as well, and much more!

Lesson/Day 3: I Am Compassionate

- Theme: Seeing things through other perspectives & God's eyes of compassion
- Main Idea: Valuing other perspectives and stories (immigrants); being able to see things from someone else's point of view.
- Explanation/Teaching Approach: The practice of seeing things through other people's eyes, from their perspective, is always a good exercise to practice, a critical life skill. We'll also bring in the idea of seeing people through God's eyes of love and compassion. We especially want to help people understand the plight of immigrants and refugees and build compassionate imagination about why someone would choose to leave their country, particularly to come to the U.S.

Objectives:
- To understand what compassion is.
- To value seeing things through other people's perspectives by trying to imagine how others think and feel, wondering about their experiences, feelings, and needs.
- To practice noticing others' needs and trying to help.

Elements:
1. Bible: Ruth (foreigner/immigrant and poor); role playing
2. Story Book: Options include stories about emigrating to the United States, stories about refugees, and stories about seeing other people around you with compassion.
3. Personal Story: people sharing what it is like to be Latinx, Asian, Black, or Indigenous in the U.S.
4. Art:
   a. God's Eye (to remind us to see others through God's eyes of compassion)
   b. Hearts of Compassion (to remind us to look for how people might need help)
5. Music: "Give Me Your Eyes" by Brandon Heath
6. Play/Activity:
   a. Contrast two games, one where people are left out/eliminated, and one where "losers" still are included in a team: "Clumps" (or "Ships and Sailors") vs. TEAM Rock/Paper/Scissors. Debrief how in one, people are left out, but in another, they are invited into a new team.

      b. Perspective games.
          i. "Newly-Friend Game" (like the newlywed game, but with a new friend you just met and have a few mins to get to know). Get to know someone, a partner. Find out their favorites, etc. (Could use Friendship Bingo to do this); then answer questions as you think THEY would answer.
          ii. Answer as the person on your right questions that you can easily see the answer to ("What color is your shirt?" Your shirt is blue, but the person to your right's shirt is pink, so you answer pink).
7. Snack: decorate a cupcake or fix a plate from a variety of options, but do it for a friend/partner, so that everyone is thinking of what someone ELSE might like (you can ask them)
8. Serve/Do: make lunches for a soup kitchen

Introduction to the Lesson and Theme

Theme: Seeing things through other perspectives & God's eyes of compassion
Main Idea: Valuing other perspectives and stories (immigrants and refugees); being able to see things from someone else's point of view. Seeing others through God's eyes of compassion.

Upfront Illustration: Glasses
Get a bunch of different glasses. Some that correct astigmatism, some that magnify everything really big, some that are different colors, some that make prisms out of all the lights, some that are 3-D. Have children volunteer to come up and put them on, and then describe how they see the world differently with them on.

Introduce the Main Ideas (say something like):
God sees things differently than we do. It's like God has on "Compassion Glasses" *(make circles with your fingers and put them up to your eyes like glasses)*.
What is compassion? Let's learn what compassion means together. Repeat after me and make some motions. Compassion means we come alongside someone *(put hand out like you're putting an arm around someone's shoulder)*, we try to understand *(put hands on head)*, and we try to help *(put hands out like you're offering a gift)*.
We need God-glasses so that we can see people with compassion like God does.

It is important to view other people and their stories with compassion. Compassion means we come alongside someone, and we try to understand them, and we try to help them as we would want someone to help us if it were happening to us. God is compassionate. God comes alongside us and tries to help us when we struggle, when we are sad and when we need help.

To help bring about God's beautiful dream of how the world was intended to be, we will have to have compassion. Today, we will practice seeing people and their stories through God's eyes of compassion. We will try to understand what others are going through and what they need, and we will try to help them.

So put on your God-glasses *(make circles with your fingers and hold them up like glasses),* so we can see the world and other people through God's eyes. We know that God loves everyone, that God has compassion, so we are going to see others today with God's eyes of compassion. *(Have children repeat and do the motions)*: Compassion means coming alongside like a friend, trying to understand, and trying to help. So, we're going to try to see things with God's eyes of compassion today with our God-glasses on!

Repeated Ideas:
- Compassion is coming alongside someone who is suffering or struggling like a friend, trying to understand, and trying to help.
- God is compassionate. God comes alongside us, tries to understand, and helps us.
- We need to look at others through God's eyes of compassion.

LEADER TIP: One nuance to the conversation around helping is consent. We want to encourage children's inclination to be a helper. AND compassion teaches us that we need to see from their perspective, which includes understanding what kind of help they might want or need, not just the kind of help we want to offer. We need to not just have good intentions; we need to also make sure we have a good impact.

Bible Story 3 | Ruth, An immigrant

Scripture Reference: The Book of Ruth, especially 1:16-18, 2:11-12

But Ruth replied, "Don't urge me to leave you or to turn back from you. Where you go I will go, and where you stay I will stay. Your people will be my people and your God my God. [17] Where you die I will die, and there I will be buried. May the Lord deal with me, be it ever so severely, if even death separates you and me." [18] When Naomi realized that Ruth was determined to go with her, she stopped urging her.

[11] Boaz replied, "I've been told all about what you have done for your mother-in-law since the death of your husband—how you left your father and mother and your homeland and came to live with a people you did not know before. [12] May the Lord repay you for what you have done. May you be richly rewarded by the Lord, the God of Israel, under whose wings you have come to take refuge."

Overview for Leader: We have immigrants to the U.S. all the time. Often, people in the U.S. look down on immigrants, especially if they don't speak English. But everyone has a story that connects us to our shared humanity. The story of Ruth reminds us of that. Ruth was an immigrant in a land that was foreign to her, at a time when many Israelites looked down on those from Moab (Ruth's country). But Ruth had a story, too, and compassion and care for others is what drove her to immigrate to Israel. Seeing Ruth's compassion connects us to our shared humanity and how all of us want to care for the ones we love and will go to great lengths to do so.

Repeated Ideas for Lesson 3 "I Am Compassionate":
- Compassion is coming alongside someone who is suffering or struggling like a friend, trying to understand, and trying to help.
- God is compassionate. God comes alongside us, tries to understand, and helps us.
- We need to look at others through God's eyes of compassion.

Storytelling Technique:
Have volunteers act out the story, pausing to put on God-glasses and seeing through God's eyes of compassion, and thinking through at different parts of the story who is having compassion, or what would compassion look like, and contrasting that to how others might be looking at them.

Introductory Statement: In our last lesson, we learned that sometimes human beings see the ways that we are different from each other and use that as an excuse to treat people unfairly. In our Bible story today, we're going to learn about Ruth, who was from the country of Moab. She was not from Israel, and many Israelites looked down on those from Moab. Because Ruth left the country where she was born and entered a new country (Israel), she is what we would call an immigrant. Sometimes we have immigrants from other countries who come to the United States, too. And sometimes, people look down on them, just because they are different. But God wants us to see differences as beautiful! God wants us to see people through God's eyes of compassion! Remember what compassion is? We're going to say this a lot today, so let's practice. Compassion is coming alongside someone like a friend, trying to understand what they need, and trying to help. So today, we're going to read the story of Ruth, and at different parts, I'm going to have us pause and put on our God-glasses. And when we put on our God-glasses, we're going to look at the people in the story with compassion. We're going to try to come alongside them like a friend, try to understand what they might need, and think of ways to help. Ready? Ok, get your God-glasses ready, and I'll tell you when it's time to put them on.

Instructions:

Leaders will ask for volunteers for the 7 roles. None of these roles have speaking parts, but they will act out the action while the narrator (who needs to be a leader) is telling the story, and the leader who is narrating will need to pause frequently to make sure they have plenty of time to act everything out and be silly and dramatic.

Roles:
Husband
Sons
Naomi
Ruth
Other daughter-in-law
Boaz

Narrator:
Naomi was an Israelite. When there was a famine, she and her husband and two sons packed up everything they had and moved to Moab. It was a long journey, and they meandered this way (to the right) and that way (back to the left) and walked and walked around and around until they got to Moab.

While in Moab, her two sons both married Moabite women. Then Naomi's husband AND her two sons ALL DIED, so only the women were left. They were very sad and cried a bit and comforted each other. And everyone around them (other students) cried and comforted each other when they heard this sad, sad news. Women in that time were vulnerable without men to protect and care and provide for them. Naomi had a problem now, because there were no men around her who could help take care of her or her daughters-in-law. So, Naomi thought about it long and hard with her best thinking face and posture and made up her mind. She decided to go by herself, an older woman alone on a journey, back to her relatives in Israel. And she would send her daughters-in-law back to their fathers' houses.

> *Let's pause and put on our God-glasses and see if we can look at Naomi with God's eyes of compassion. Compassion means (say it with me) coming alongside someone like a friend, trying to understand what they need, and trying to help.*
> *Naomi has just lost her husband and both her sons, all the men in the family, and she's in a faraway land, where she doesn't have any other family.*
> - *So, I wonder what Naomi would want us to understand about how she feels, what she's going through, what she's afraid of?*
> - *I wonder what Naomi might need?*

Let's continue with our story. Naomi told the Moabite daughters-in-law to go back to their fathers' houses, so they could have protection and food and supplies and stuff. Ruth was one of the daughters-in-law, and Ruth had COMPASSION for Naomi; she tried to come alongside Naomi, to understand what she needed, and to try to help. She decided she could not leave Naomi all alone to fend for herself. She got down on her knees and took Naomi by the hand and promised to go with her anywhere, that she would make a home among Naomi's people, the Israelites, and follow Israel's God. Naomi tried to shake her off and told her to go back home to her family, but Ruth clung to her and wouldn't leave her side.

So, Naomi and Ruth made the journey back to Israel, and walked, and marched, and hopped and skipped. It was a long journey.

When Naomi and Ruth arrived in Israel, they had nothing. They had no food, and they were hungry! But there was a law in Israel that helped the poor: the law stated that those who owned fields should not harvest all the grain, but should leave some grain for the poor to collect. So, Ruth got on her work clothes and tied up her hair, and got a bag, and she went to work in a nearby field, picking grain so she and Naomi could eat. And it was hard work, and her back hurt a little, so she had to stop and stretch her back, and then she had to stop and take a drink, and it was so hot and the sun was so bright, but she did it!

Now, let's look at Ruth for a moment. She was an immigrant and a foreigner who's not from the area. She doesn't know the ways or customs. She may not have spoken the language very well. She lost her husband, moved away from all of her other family, and is responsible now for caring for her mother-in-law. She doesn't know anyone else working in that field. She doesn't have anyone to stand up for her or protect her, and sometimes women who were working alone got hurt by other workers while trying to work in the fields. So, it could have been a bit dangerous for her.

I wonder what others would have thought about Ruth, a Moabite and a foreigner? The Israelites thought they were not supposed to mingle with Moabites like Ruth and may have looked down on her.

Now Let's put on our God-glasses and see if we can look at Ruth with God's eyes of compassion. Compassion means (say it with me) coming alongside someone like a friend, trying to understand what they need, and trying to help.
- *I wonder what Ruth would want us to understand about how she feels? I wonder what she might be worried about?*
- *I wonder what kind of help Ruth might need right now?*

Let's continue with our story. While Ruth was in the field working, she met the owner of the field, a guy named Boaz. Boaz saw Ruth with COMPASSION. He knew she needed protection and provision like supplies and food and stuff, so he told all his workers very sternly, shaking his fingers at them, to take care of Ruth and protect her while she was working, and he made sure she had all she needed. He ran and got her some water, and then he ran and got her some food, and he told her to take a rest in the shade. And he was kind to her.

So, Ruth and Naomi were able to survive because of Boaz's generosity, because Boaz saw them with eyes of COMPASSION, and came alongside them like a friend, tried to understand what they needed, and tried to help. And also because the Lord was watching out for them.... Because it turns out there was a reason the Lord led Ruth to THAT field. Boaz was a close relative of Naomi's. The law also said, basically, that if someone in your family found themselves in hard circumstances, the closest relative could do what was needed to take care of you. So, Boaz married Ruth and took care of her and Naomi. And Ruth and Boaz had a little baby named Obed and had a good life, and Naomi was thrilled and happy again!

"Wondering" Questions:
- Naomi lost her husband and both her sons while living in a faraway land. She didn't really have anyone to help her. I wonder how we would see Naomi through God's eyes of compassion (compassion means coming alongside someone like a friend, trying to understand them, and trying to help them)? I wonder what Naomi would want us to understand? I wonder how Naomi might need help?
- Ruth was an immigrant and a foreigner. She may not have spoken the language of the Israelites. She had lost her husband, moved away from her other family, and had to take care of her mother-in-law. I wonder how we would see Ruth through God's eyes of compassion? I wonder what Ruth might want us to understand? I wonder how Ruth might need help?
- In the story, Boaz and Naomi both tell Ruth to stay in Boaz's field, or otherwise, she might be mistreated. Israelites thought that they were not supposed to mingle with Moabites, and it seems like they probably looked down on Moabites like Ruth. I wonder what others thought of Ruth, an immigrant, and a foreigner?

Summary Statement (summarize main idea & connect back to theme):
- Ruth saw Naomi with compassion (she saw her suffering, and she tried to understand and help).
- Boaz saw Ruth with compassion (he saw her hardships and struggles, and he tried to understand and help).
- God sees us with compassion and asks that we see others with God's eyes of compassion as well.

Story Book 3

There are several options here.

First, there are stories that help children understand immigration from the Southern Border of the United States. *Dreamers* and *La Frontera* address this. *Dreamers* is probably more appropriate for younger children.

Second, there are stories that help children understand what it means to be a refugee. While some immigration happens because people are pulled toward a new country with new opportunities, other immigration happens because people are pushed out of their countries due to wars or other dangers. They often live in refugee camps before immigrating to another country. *What is a Refugee?* is a very straightforward and easy to understand explanation of displaced peoples. *Lost and Found Cat* follows the true story of a refugee family losing and finding their cat again and is really about kindness. It also addresses some of the dangers refugees, particularly Syrian refugees, have faced in order to immigrate to other countries. *Salma the Syrian Chef* is also about a Syrian refugee in Canada, and some of the frustrations of trying to live in a new country, while also highlighting kindness.

Dreamers (elementary)

Overview for Leaders:
This book is not about Dreamers in the sense of those who were children of immigrants born in the United States, but just about having a dream for a better life, and making their home in the United States, and their experiences trying to settle in a different country.

Repeated Ideas for Lesson 3 "I Am Compassionate":
- Compassion is coming alongside someone who is suffering or struggling like a friend, trying to understand, and trying to help.
- God is compassionate. God comes alongside us, tries to understand, and helps us.
- We need to look at others through God's eyes of compassion.

Introductory Statement:
We learned that Ruth in the Bible was an immigrant, and how she immigrated to Israel because she loved and wanted to help her mother-in-law. Sometimes people in the United States wonder why people are immigrating at our Southern Border with Mexico. Some people say they should go back and not enter the U.S. We are going to look at people with God's eyes of compassion (which means we come alongside them like a friend, and we try to understand, and we try to help), so this story, "Dreamers," may help us. It is the story about a mother and son who immigrated to the United States from Mexico, and a little bit about their experiences. Let's put on God-glasses, so we can look at them with God's eyes of compassion as we hear this story.

Read the Story: *Dreamers* by Yuyi Morales, Neil Porter Books, 2018

"Wondering" Questions:
- I wonder what it would be like to leave my country that I live in right now and move to a whole different country that spoke a language I didn't speak?
- I wonder what I might need if I didn't speak the language everyone else spoke? I wonder what kind of things would help me?
- I wonder how someone could be a friend to me if I didn't understand the language everyone else spoke? I wonder what we could do to help someone who didn't speak our language and needed help? I wonder how you can communicate without using words that you are a friendly person who wants to help?

Summary Statement (summarize main idea of story & connect back to theme):
This story talks about some of the things that were hard about immigrating (moving into) the United States, especially when the mother didn't speak the language. When we use compassion to look at that mother and son and their experiences and struggles, it means that we think about how we could be a friend to them, how we could help them. Now that we understand the experience of immigrants to the United States a little bit better, we might know a bit more about what might help them.

La Frontera (elementary)

Overview for Leaders:
This book is about migration from Central America to a new land (the United States). It touches on some of the reasons for leaving home, some of the feelings there, some of the hardships of the journey, some of the experiences in getting settled, and the ways kindness and inclusion helped. The back of the book offers pictures of this true story and more facts about migration and immigrant experiences.

Repeated Ideas for Lesson 3 "I Am Compassionate":
- Compassion is coming alongside someone who is suffering or struggling like a friend, trying to understand, and trying to help.
- God is compassionate. God comes alongside us, tries to understand, and helps us.
- We need to look at others through God's eyes of compassion.

Introductory Statement:
We learned that Ruth in the Bible was an immigrant, and how she immigrated to Israel because she loved and wanted to help her mother-in-law. Sometimes people in the United States wonder why people are immigrating at our Southern Border with Mexico. Some people say they should go back and not enter the U.S. We are going to look at people with God's eyes of compassion (which means we come alongside them like a friend, and we try to understand, and we try to help), so this story may help us. It is the story about a father and son who immigrated to the United States from Mexico and a little bit about their experiences. Let's put on God-glasses, so we can look at them with God's eyes of compassion as we hear this story.

Read the Story: *La Frontera: My Journey with Papa* by Deborah Mills, Barefoot Books, 2018

"Wondering" Questions:
- I wonder what it would be like to be away from your mama and siblings for so long? I wonder what it would be like to sleep on the ground with rocks and bugs? I wonder what it would be like to go to school without knowing anyone or speaking the language?
- Compassion is when you come alongside someone like a friend, and try to understand, and try to help. I wonder what Alfredo needs help with? I wonder what looking at Alfredo with eyes of compassion would mean? I wonder if you saw someone with compassion in this story?

Summary Statement (summarize main idea of story & connect back to theme):
When we see people with God's eyes of compassion, it means we try to come alongside them like a friend, we try to understand what they're going through and what they need, and we try to help. There are many, many people in this world that are going through struggles and hardship, and they need compassion.

What is a Refugee (Pre-K/K, ages 3-7 and up)

Overview for Leaders:
This book talks in straightforward and simple terms about what a refugee is, and some of the reasons they might have for leaving their home countries.

Repeated Ideas for Lesson 3 "I Am Compassionate":
- Compassion is coming alongside someone who is suffering or struggling like a friend, trying to understand, and trying to help.
- God is compassionate. God comes alongside us, tries to understand, and helps us.
- We need to look at others through God's eyes of compassion.

Introductory Statement:
Have you ever heard of a refugee? A refugee is someone who is seeking refuge, which is a word that can mean a safe place. They are usually coming from another country that isn't safe for them anymore, and so they have to leave, and they are seeking a new home where they can be safe. We're going to read a book that tells a little bit about refugees and what their experiences are like. This book talks about what a refugee is, and some of the reasons people might have to leave their home countries. Let's put on God-glasses, so we can look at them with God's eyes of compassion as we hear this story (Remember compassion means, we come alongside someone like a friend, and try to understand them, and try to help).

Read the Story: *What is a Refugee?* by Elise Gravel, Schwartz & Wade, 2019

"Wondering" Questions:
- I wonder if any of you have ever moved before? I wonder what was fun about that? I wonder what was hard about moving for you?
- I wonder what it would be like if we were in danger here and had to leave and travel to a new home? Sometimes, refugees can only take with them what they can put in their backpack. I wonder what you would take with you if you could only take a few things?
- I wonder what refugees might need when living in camps, since they couldn't take everything with them? I wonder how we could help them?

Summary Statement (summarize main idea of story & connect back to theme):
Refugees are people just like you and me, and they are made in God's image, and God loves them so very much. This is one of the messes that human beings caused in going to war and being mean to each other. It's a big mess to fix, and it might be hard to face, but remember,

Living God's Dream **93**

we can be brave to face hard problems and help fix them with God's help. God has compassion for refugees, which means God wants to come alongside them like a friend, and care for them, and help them. If we are looking at refugees with God's eyes of compassion, we will want to understand what they need and try to help. So now that we know about refugees, we can try to help them. There are some organizations that are already helping refugees, and we can work with those organizations to help!

LEADER TIP: This might be a good place to research organizations that help refugees in your own area. There are refugee resettlement agencies that help get refugees settled in the United States, and they often partner with groups to set up new homes for incoming refugees. They sometimes need donations of clothing, furniture, bedding, etc. to set up new homes. World Relief is a national refugee resettlement agency. The Diocese of Atlanta partners with a local agency called New American Pathways to resettle refugees. There are also non-profit groups that help on the frontlines of the wars that cause refugee crises. Preemptive Love Coalition is one. They have many ways to help. One way you might support refugees is to raffle off an item (such as a stuffed animal made by refugees...you can find one at the Preemptive Love Coalition's website). Have the children bring any number of coins each day of your lesson series, and for each coin they donate, write their name on a raffle ticket, and draw a name at the end of the series to see who wins the stuffed animal. All the proceeds from the raffle can go to support refugees.

Lost and Found Cat (Pre-K/K and elementary, ages 4-8 and up)

Overview for Leaders:
This story is a true story of a family's escape from danger in Iraq with their cat. The cat gets lost, but through the kindness of strangers and the connection of the internet, the cat is reunited with the family again. It demonstrates compassion as the helpers treat the refugees and their cat how they would want to be treated, and it helps children understand the experience of refugees, through the common experience of loving a pet.

Repeated Ideas for Lesson 3 "I Am Compassionate":
- Compassion is coming alongside someone who is suffering or struggling like a friend, trying to understand, and trying to help.
- God is compassionate. God comes alongside us, tries to understand, and helps us.
- We need to look at others through God's eyes of compassion.

Introductory Statement:
This story took place in another country, and in a culture that is different in many ways than American culture in the United States. But in some ways, we are the same…this family has pets, wants to have a safe place to live and love each other, and we all need help and kindness sometimes. Let's put on God-glasses, so we can look at them with God's eyes of compassion as we hear this story, to try to understand this family and what they might need, and how we can help others like them.

Read the Story: *Lost and Found Cat: The True Story of Kunkush's Incredible Journey*
by Doug Kuntz and Amy Shrodes, illustrated by Sue Cornelison, Crown Books for Young Readers, 2017

"Wondering" Questions:
- I wonder if you have any pets and how you feel about those pets?
- I wonder what it would be like if you lost a pet? If I lost a pet, I would hope someone would help me get it back! This family lost more than just their pet. I wonder how we can help families like them to get the things they need, to help them replace some of the things they lost?

- If you were in that situation where you had to leave your home and leave most of your belongings, and maybe even lost your pet, I wonder what you would want? I wonder how we could give refugees some of those things for them that you would want for yourself?

Summary Statement (summarize main idea of story & connect back to theme):
Refugees are people just like you and me, and they are made in God's image, and God loves them so very much. This is one of the messes that human beings caused in going to war and being mean to each other. It's a big mess to fix, and it might be hard to face, but remember, we can be brave to face hard problems and help fix them with God's help. God has compassion for refugees, which means God wants to come alongside them like a friend, and care for them, and help them. If we are looking at refugees with God's eyes of compassion, we will want to understand what they need and try to help. So, now that we know about refugees, we can try to help them. There are some organizations that are already helping refugees, and we can work with those organizations to help!

Salma the Syrian Chef (elementary)

Overview for Leaders:
This book is about a Syrian refugee family who settle in Canada, and their experience of trying to make a home in a new place, while missing their old home country. Salma tries to make a dish from Syria for her mother to cheer her up. It depicts the struggles and resilience of the refugee family and the help, kindness, and compassion of friends.

Repeated Ideas for Lesson 3 "I Am Compassionate":
- Compassion is coming alongside someone who is suffering or struggling like a friend, trying to understand, and trying to help.
- God is compassionate. God comes alongside us, tries to understand, and helps us.
- We need to look at others through God's eyes of compassion.

Introductory Statement:
Have you ever heard of a refugee? A refugee is someone who is seeking refuge, which is a word that can mean a safe place. They are usually coming from another country that isn't safe for them anymore, and so they have to leave, and they are seeking a new home where they can be safe. The story we're going to read is about a mother and daughter who were from Syria, and they had to take refuge from danger in the country of Canada, and about their experience of trying to get settled in a new and very different place. I hope you'll notice some of the things that were hard, and also some of the kindness that different people in the book show. Pay attention to who is kind and has compassion. Remember, compassion is coming alongside someone as a friend, trying to understand what they need, and trying to help. So, look for those who show compassion. And let's put on God-glasses, so we can look at them with God's eyes of compassion as we hear this story, to try to understand this family and what they might need, and how we can help others like them.

Read the Story: *Selma the Syrian Chef* by Danny Ramadan, illustrated by Anna Bron, Annick Press, 2020

"Wondering" Questions:
- I wonder what it would be like to miss your home and be glad you are safe in a new country at the same time?
- I wonder what you noticed that was a struggle for Salma, or something that was hard or frustrating for her?
- I wonder where you saw someone showing compassion in this story (someone who came alongside as a friend, tried to understand, and tried to help)?

Summary Statement (summarize main idea of story & connect back to theme):
There are so many wonderful examples of compassion in this story! There are so many times when a friend came alongside, tried to understand, and tried to help. And even though some things were still hard, compassionate friends definitely helped a lot. Things in life can sometimes be really hard, and we all need friends who show us compassion when we need it most! So, let's keep remembering that we can be the person that helps, that makes a struggle easier for someone. We can be the one that makes their day easier, their world a little better, when we show compassion!

The Invisible Boy (Pre-K/K)

Overview for Leaders: *The Invisible Boy* by Trudy Ludwig, is about a boy that feels unseen at school until a new student arrives and is able to appreciate who he is.

Repeated Ideas for Lesson 3 "I Am Compassionate":
- Compassion is coming alongside someone who is suffering or struggling like a friend, trying to understand, and trying to help.
- God is compassionate. God comes alongside us, tries to understand, and helps us.
- We need to look at others through God's eyes of compassion.

Introductory Statement:
This is a story that is about something that most of us have been able to relate to at least some time in our life. It is about a boy named Bryan who feels like he is invisible when he's at school, which makes him lonely and sad. But then one day, a new boy shows up at the school that Bryan notices is a little different and special. Maybe this new boy can show some compassion to Bryan and see the ways that Bryan is special.

Read the Story: Read *The Invisible Boy* by Trudy Ludwig, illustrated by Patrice Barton, Knopf Books for Young Readers, 2013

"Wondering" Questions:
- I wonder if Bryan was happy at school before Justin arrived. Was he excited to go to school in the mornings? What did he tell his parents when he got home at the end of the day? I wonder what it feels like to not be noticed.
- I wonder how Bryan felt different after he met Justin. Why was Justin able to "see" Bryan when no one else could? I wonder how Bryan's life changed after he met Justin. I wonder if Justin and Bryan became best friends.
- I wonder if there are people around me who feel invisible, just like Bryan. I wonder if there is anything I can do to "see" them? I wonder if there are new friends around me that I just haven't noticed yet!

Summary Statement (summarize main idea of the story & connect back to the theme):
Everyone that God has made has value, but for some reason it is easier to notice some people more than others. Just like in the story, there are people in our lives, like Bryan,

who are really special and fun to be with, but we have to slow down and pay attention to be able to see them. Slowing down and noticing those people may result in having a new friend, but even when it doesn't, it will definitely result in helping that person feel the love that God has for them.

Personal Story 3 | Stories of Immigrants

Black, Asian, or Latinx in the U.S.:

Overview for Leaders:
These personal stories are intended to make real some of the ideas about Ruth's experience and the experience of immigration. Telling stories of real, wonderful people who have had the experience of immigrating fosters compassion. This story is intended to be about the experience of someone who is coming from a majority Black country (or from a majority Asian country or from a majority Latinx country) to the United States, to highlight what it might be like to see the U.S. with different eyes.

Repeated Ideas for Lesson 3 "I Am Compassionate":
- Compassion is coming alongside someone who is suffering or struggling like a friend, trying to understand, and trying to help.
- God is compassionate. God comes alongside us, tries to understand, and helps us.
- We need to look at others through God's eyes of compassion.

Introductory Statement:
Remember how Ruth left her country to help her mother-in-law? She left everyone she knew and had to figure out how to get by and make a living in a whole new place with different customs and ways of doing things! Have you ever wondered what it would be like to leave the country you grew up in and go live somewhere else totally different? I wonder what you would need to thrive in a new place? Compassionate friends and helpers to help you navigate a whole new way of living, maybe? We're going to hear a story about someone who did exactly that: they left the country where they were born, and they came to live in the United States, and they're going to share with us what that experience was like. We want to listen to this story with our God-glasses on…we want to see and hear with compassion, listening for ways we can come alongside people who might be having an experience like this, so that we can understand and help.

Share the Story:
(You can invite someone from your context to share a story, or you can also visit the Diocese of Atlanta website under Resources>Education & Formation, and click on the section for Dismantling Racism curriculum to see more video stories there.)

Questions for the Storyteller to consider:
- What were the major differences you noticed in coming from one country to the U.S.? What was most exciting or intriguing? What was most challenging? What did you like? What did you miss?
- When did you experience a lack of compassion or discrimination? How did that affect you? How would you describe your feelings about that? What did you tell yourself as you processed those feelings that helped?
- When did you experience the compassion and help of other people? How did that affect you? How would you describe your feelings about that experience of receiving compassion and help?
- Where did you experience God in all of this?
- What were your biggest learnings?
- What would you want children from the U.S. to know or to do that would help those who are immigrating to the U.S.?

Summary Statement (summarize main idea of story & connect back to theme):
In our Bible story, we learned about how Ruth was a stranger in a place far from her home. Today, we heard about how coming to a new place is hard, especially when the food is different, and the language is different, and you don't know anyone! During these times, it is important to find compassionate people. WE can be those compassionate people! When we meet new friends who have come from another place, we can be compassionate and come alongside them like a friend, and try to understand and try to help. I hope you heard some ideas about how we might be able to do that and show compassion to those who are navigating a new place.

Art 3

Option 1: God's Eyes

Supplies:
- Craft sticks (popsicle sticks), 2 per person
- Yarn
- Scissors

Overview for Leaders: The resulting craft project, which loosely resembles an eye, will help serve as a reminder to look at others through God's eyes of compassion.

Repeated Ideas for Lesson 3 "I Am Compassionate":
- Compassion is coming alongside someone who is suffering or struggling like a friend, trying to understand, and trying to help.
- God is compassionate. God comes alongside us, tries to understand, and helps us.
- We need to look at others through God's eyes of compassion.

Introductory Statement: We are called to see others through God's eyes of compassion. The craft we will create today will remind us to look at other people with God's eyes of compassion. Remember what compassion is? Let's say it together: Compassion is coming alongside someone like a friend, trying to understand what they need, and trying to help. This craft will look like an eye when we're done, so it will remind us to see people through God's eyes of compassion.

Instructions:
- Explain to the children how to make a God's Eye. If you need instructions, you can look in the resource section of the Diocese of Atlanta website or search the internet for God's Eye instructions.
- Show them how the finished product kind of looks like an eye, and how these are traditionally called God's eyes.
- Put them at tables and let them go to work as adults help.
- As you are working, talk about how we are called to see other people through God's eyes of compassion. Hold yours up to your eye and "view" people with it and wonder what God would see as God looks at each person. (God sees each person in love, comes alongside as a friend, tries to understand them, and help them.) So, when you look at each person through your God's eye, say something about how they are so loved and wonderful, list something beautiful about their personality.

- When someone asks for help, hold up your God's eye, and say something like, "When I look at you with God's eyes of compassion, I see someone who is loved, and it makes me want to help you… I'm happy to help you with what you need."
- Have the children practice seeing each other through their God's eyes, practicing seeing how beloved they are, practicing helping.

Summary Statement (summarize main idea of art & connect back to the theme):
Today we are learning about compassion and how to be compassionate. God is always compassionate to us, so we can think about that when we are learning to be compassionate to others. Compassion means coming alongside someone like a friend, trying to understand them and what they need, and trying to help. When we use God's eyes to see each other, it makes the world a much better and more loving place… When we see through God's eyes, we see that each person is someone God loves ENORMOUSLY, and we try to understand what they need, and we try to help. If everyone did that all the time, we would bring God's dream for us to earth. We don't always do that perfectly, but we can try, and the more we practice, the better we'll get. So, practice seeing others through your God's Eye…seeing them as God sees them, with love and compassion, and try to understand what they're going through, what they need, and how you can help!

Option 2: Hearts of Compassion

Supplies:
- At least 1 copy of hearts page per child (total of 4 hearts per child)
- Crayons and/or markers
- Scissors
- Glue sticks
- Hole punch
- Craft string or yarn

Overview for Leaders: This craft activity will give the children a chance to notice the ways people around them need help and then think of ways they might help them. That may be an action, or even kind words. The final product will be a hanging heart ornament.

Repeated Ideas for Lesson 3 "I Am Compassionate":
- Compassion is coming alongside someone who is suffering or struggling like a friend, trying to understand, and trying to help.
- God is compassionate. God comes alongside us, tries to understand, and helps us.
- We need to look at others through God's eyes of compassion.

Introductory Statement:
Today we have been talking about what it means to be compassionate. In the same way that God has shown compassion to us, we have been called to come alongside others and try to understand who they are and what they need. When we show compassion and try to understand them and their circumstances, we will be better able to offer them what they need. In this art project, we will make Hearts of Compassion that we can take home and display as a way to remind ourselves to show compassion and offer help to those around us.

Instructions:
- Talk a little about the theme for the day, reminding the children about what it looks like to be compassionate. We can show compassion by coming alongside someone who is struggling and offer to help. We can share words of encouragement as well as actions.
- Allow the children to think of ways they have seen people around them struggling. Examples: a mother has her arms full with her children and is struggling to open a door, a new kid at school is lonely, their brother is afraid of the dark, a friend forgot to bring a snack, etc.

- Invite the children to make "Hearts of Compassion" to think about how they might come alongside these people who are struggling and offer them help.
- Pass out a copy of one heart page per child, each page containing 4 hearts. The final product can be made with more hearts but looks best with at least 4. If a child wants to add more, feel free to provide them with more hearts!
- On the left side of each heart, the children will write down a way they have seen someone struggling. On the right-hand side, they will write down a way they can help. Example: right side- my brother is afraid of the dark, left side- I can let him sleep with my stuffed animal.
- Once they have written down the ways they see people struggle and how they might help, give them time to decorate the hearts and cut them out.
- When they are done filling them out, have the children cut out and fold each heart in half and use a glue stick to attach it to the half of another heart. They should do this with each heart, creating a sort of ring which will result in a 3-dimensional heart.
- Using a hole puncher, help the children add a hole to the top of the heart.
- Loop a piece of string through the hole at the top of the heart so that the heart can hang in their homes, or you can attach to a hanger to make a mobile for the classroom and remind them to show compassion to others.
- Allow the children a chance to share some of the ways that they can show compassion by coming alongside others and help them.

LEADER TIP: Younger children will likely benefit from having pre-cut hearts, or even hearts that are larger than the ones on the provided printing sheet. You will likely also need to help them write in the ways they notice people struggling and how they might help.

Summary Statement (summarize main idea of art & connect back to the theme):
God calls us to have compassion for others by looking for those who might be struggling and offering our help. Sometimes that means doing something that is really challenging for us, and other times it's more simple, but every time we care for someone in this way, we are showing love and bringing glory to God. Every time we reach out to someone, we are being brave, fixing messes, and loving each other like God wants us to. These Hearts of Compassion remind us that, no matter what age we are, we can always find a way to help someone who is struggling.

LESSON 3

Living God's Dream **107**

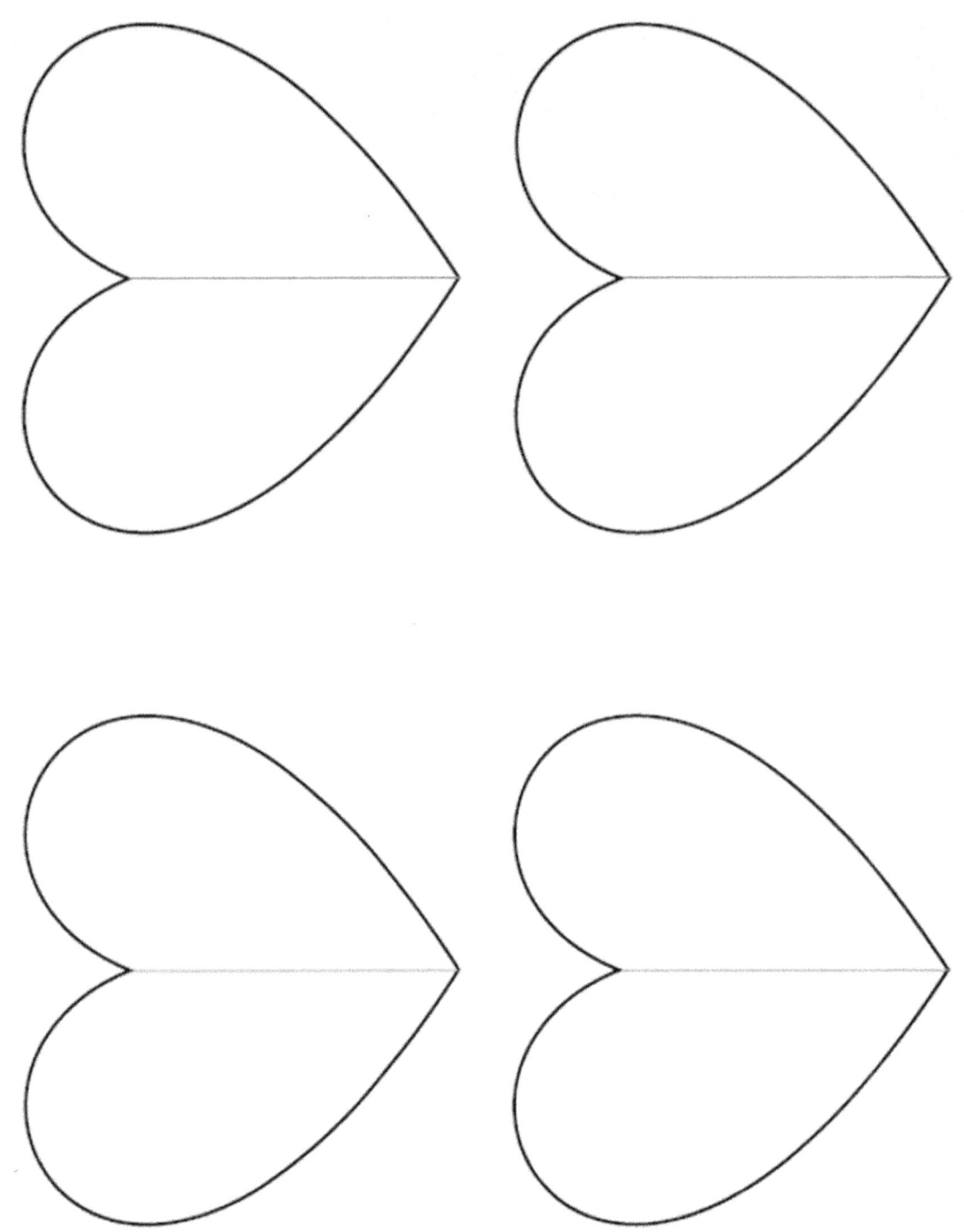

*This page is reproducible.

Music 3

Song(s): "Give Me Your Eyes"

Song #1: "Give Me Your Eyes" by Brandon Heath and Jason Ingram, Reunion music, 2008 from Album *What If We*. This song can be licensed through CCLI, or you can find sheet music through Christianbook Distributors.

Overview for Leaders:
This song asks God to give us God's eyes, so that we can really see people with love, and we can pay attention to what they might need.

Repeated Ideas for Lesson 3 "I Am Compassionate":
- Compassion is coming alongside someone who is suffering or struggling like a friend, trying to understand, and trying to help.
- God is compassionate. God comes alongside us, tries to understand, and helps us.
- We need to look at others through God's eyes of compassion.

Introductory Statement to Singing the Song:
This song is a prayer asking for God to give us God's eyes of compassion, to see people through God's eyes of compassion. In the song, the singer starts to really notice the people around him and wonder about their stories and what they're going through and what they might be dealing with. A girl who's smiling but is really sad. A man who's dressed up for work, but he actually just lost his job. The singer wonders why he's never noticed these people before…he's never paid attention to them, and he asks God to give him God's eyes to really see them with compassion, to see what they need, to care about them, and to try to help.

Special Instructions/Motions:
As a leader, you can choreograph motions ahead of time and teach them to the children, or you can just have the children do interpretative dance/motions to the lyrics that they make up, and then ask them why they might have chosen those motions, and what they're trying to convey.

If you want to choreograph motions in advance, here are some ideas for the chorus:
- When it mentions eyes, have the children point to their eyes, or make circles around their eyes.
- When it mentions "everything I can see," you could have them put their hand above their eyes, like they're searching or looking.

- When it mentions love, they could cross their arms across their chest like they're giving themselves a hug.
- When it mentions broken-hearted, they could make a heart shape out of their hands and hold it to their heart.
- When it mentions reach, they could spread their arms out wide.
- When it mentions heart again, they could cross their hands over their heart.

Summary Statement (summarize main idea & connect back to the theme):
God sees people through eyes of compassion. Compassion is coming alongside someone like a friend, trying to understand, caring about them, and trying to help. Sometimes we forget to really look at people and see them as friends made in God's image. We just go about our day, and don't really pay attention to others or even think about how they're doing and what they need. So, we need to pray for God's eyes, to see people with compassion, so that we can care for them and help them. That's our prayer today, that God would give us GOD's eyes to see other people, so we can be compassionate and help!

Play/Activity 3

Inclusion vs Exclusion Games

Supplies:
No supplies needed, just children to play the games!

Overview for Leaders:
In this segment, you'll lead the children in playing two types of games. In the first type of game, children who lose or get "out" will be excluded from continuing to play. They'll have to sit along the side and just watch until the game ends. In the second type of game, children who lose will be included and invited to be part of the winning team, and to continue participating in a new way. At the end we'll debrief these two ways of playing games, and then talk about how life is like that too. Sometimes things in life are set up to exclude people, but there's another way to live life. We don't have to play those exclusion games. We can still include people.

Repeated Ideas for Lesson 3 "I Am Compassionate":
- Compassion is coming alongside someone who is suffering or struggling like a friend, trying to understand, and trying to help.
- God is compassionate. God comes alongside us, tries to understand, and helps us.
- We need to look at others through God's eyes of compassion.

Introductory Statement: When we see people through God's eyes, we will see them with compassion. Compassion doesn't exclude people or turn away from them, but rather, compassion means coming alongside others as friends. Compassion includes people, because compassion helps us understand that we need each other, and we need community. Today we're going to play some games, and then at the end, we're going to talk about how those games might show us something about COMPASSION. So, pay attention!

Instructions:
Play two games with the children: "Clumps" or "Ships and Sailors" and then a team version of Rock/Paper/Scissors

Game 1: "Clumps" (or "Ships and Sailors")
For Clumps, have the children mingle until you call a number. Then the children get in a group or "clump" of that number. Groups of the wrong number of children are out and have

Living God's Dream

to go sit apart from those who are still playing. For example, if you call "seven," groups of 6 or 8 are out. Children who don't have a group are also out.

For "Ships and Sailors," this is a variation on "Clumps." The leader calls out the names, and the children have to know how many will be in the group and make the appropriate motions or they're out.
- Group of 1: "Swab the deck" (make a mopping motion)
- Group of 1: "Beached Whale" (everyone lies on their stomach on the ground and makes whale noises)
- Group of 2: "Lighthouse" (two children face each other and put their hands together, making a point, and then rotate around in a circle, like a lighthouse light)
- Group of 3: "Man Overboard" (two children hold hands across from each other, making the "boat," and the third child is in between them, looking for a man overboard)
- Group of 4: "Row to Shore" (four children stand in a line facing the same way, one in front of the other, like they are in a rowboat, and start making rowing motions)
- Group of 5: "5 Sailors Pointing North" (5 children stand in a circle and point up to the ceiling)

Game 2: Team Rock/Paper/Scissors
(You could also do different versions of this game: Superman/Lex Luthor/Kryptonite or Mouse/Cow/Elephant, etc.)
- Explain Rock/Paper/Scissors… show the motions for each, and explain that rock beats scissors, scissors beats paper, and paper beats rock. Explain that they'll keep their hand in a fist until they say "shoot" (they'll say "rock, paper, scissors, shoot") and that both players will reveal their choice of rock, paper, or scissors at the same time, and then see who wins.
- Everyone finds a partner and plays a game of "rock/paper/scissors." Whoever wins acquires as their teammate and cheerleader the one that loses. So, the one who lost is now on the winning team, and their job is to follow their team leader (the winner who is still playing) around and cheer them on. They will hold their team leader's shoulders and form a single file line, holding shoulders of the one in front of them, as more people are incorporated into the team. They will continue playing until only one person has won all the games and has incorporated all the teammates into one giant team.

Debrief/Discussion:
- We just played two types of games. In the first game, when you lost, you had to sit out and not participate. In the second game, when you lost, you got to be part of a new team and still got to participate. I wonder which game you thought was more fun? I wonder which

game you think would be more fun for those who don't win right away, who get out pretty early?

- In life there will be times when the way we do things is set up to exclude people, but I always think it's better to include people. Like sometimes, we have try-outs for a sports team, and as you get older, not everyone gets picked for the team. They are excluded. I wonder how we might include them in new ways (maybe not in the sports team, because we don't always make the rules about that). I wonder how we can still make sure they know they are still loved and valued? (Maybe you could invite them to play a neighborhood game together.)

Summary Statement (summarize main idea of activity & connect back to the theme): To me, the second game is more fun, especially if you don't always win. The second game is a compassionate way to play. Compassion means we come alongside people like a friend, and we try to understand what they're feeling and what they're going through, and we try to help. If we have compassion, we will see someone who is left out, and we will come alongside them like a friend, and understand what it feels like to be left out and try to help by inviting them to be a part of the group. Compassion is inclusive, meaning it includes people; it invites people to be a part of the community. Compassion understands that we human beings need each other, and it invites people in. When we see people through God's eyes of compassion, we know that being left out is not fun, and we know that being invited in makes us feel special. So, to be compassionate, we need to be including other people, and making sure no one gets left out.

Perspective Games

Supplies
Paper and pencils/markers/crayons

Overview for Leaders:
Included here are several different "perspective" games, which require children to think about something from the perspective of another person, in order to help build their compassion skills.

Repeated Ideas for Lesson 3 "I Am Compassionate":
- Compassion is coming alongside someone who is suffering or struggling like a friend, trying to understand, and trying to help.
- God is compassionate. God comes alongside us, tries to understand, and helps us.
- We need to look at others through God's eyes of compassion.

Introductory Statement:
Compassion means being able to understand someone. It means being able to see things from their perspective and point of view. We're going to play some games that help us practice seeing things from someone else's point of view.

Instructions
Choose one or more games to work on seeing things from other perspectives.

Newly "Friend" Game
- This is a variation of the Newly-Wed Game. Put the children in pairs. For younger children, give them the questions in advance of things they'll want to learn about each other. For older children, you might give them 5-7 minutes to just learn everything they can about their partner's likes and dislikes, about their family, about what they like to do, etc.
- Give the children paper and pencils/markers and instruct them to write down how they think their PARTNER would answer the question on one side, and how THEY would answer the question on the other side. You might want to label the sides for them. For younger children, they can draw pictures.
- Have the children sit back-to-back in their pairs.
- Ask the questions, and then have them write down the answers. Ask questions like:
  - Favorite color
  - Favorite dessert

- ○ Number of siblings
- ○ Middle name
- ○ Sweet or sour
- ○ What are they involved in outside of school (like, soccer, scouts, piano, etc.)
- ○ Birth month
- ○ Favorite subject in school
- Have them reveal to each other if they got it right, and then ask for volunteers to share with the large group if they got it right.

Who Am I?

The purpose of this game is to practice seeing things from another person's point of view.

- Have the children sit in a circle.
- Give them instructions about the "RULE" which tells them "who they are," because they'll answer questions based on another person's perspective. If the "Rule" is that they are the person to their right, they will need to answer questions as if they are the person to their right.
- Ask questions one person at a time, of an individual child, about things they can see about the other children, like:
  - ○ Susie, what color shirt are you wearing? *(She will answer as if she is the person to her right, or whatever the "rule" is).*
  - ○ Roberto, what color eyes do you have?
  - ○ Tobias, what color hair do you have?
  - ○ Monique, what kind of shoes are you wearing?
- To make it harder, you can have them answer as if they were someone sitting farther away, like the person 3 people to their right, etc.
- For an added element, you can have a child volunteer (for older children) or an adult leave the room while you give the "Rule" and instructions about who the children are, and then have the volunteer come back in and ask questions to see if the volunteer can guess the "Rule" (everyone is answering as if they are two people to the left, etc.).
- For an additional round, you could also give them several minutes to learn everyone's favorite color or favorite ice cream flavor and play again from their memory (not what they can immediately see) about what everyone likes.

Debrief/Discussion

I wonder what it was like to think about answering those questions as if you were someone else? We asked questions about things we could see on the outside, but I wonder if we asked questions about things we couldn't see (like favorite color or favorite snack food) what that would be like?

I wonder what we would need to do to know someone more than just on the outside? How would we find out those things about a person that we can't just see?

Summary Statement (summarize main idea of activity and connect back to theme)
Compassion means coming alongside someone like a friend, and learning about them, so you can understand their perspective, their way of seeing things. When you have compassion and learn about people, it means you can understand what it's like to be them (not completely, but you can try to understand a little bit more than you did). These games helped us practice what it was like to see the world from someone else's point of view. The ability to do that is something that helps us be more compassionate, so it's good practice to think about how *others* might be thinking, or what life might be like for *other* people. Good job!

Snack 3 | Serving Another

Supplies:
Whatever snacks you are serving, but just have a variety (chips/carbs, fruits, veggies, etc.)

Overview for Leaders:
Compassion is coming alongside someone else like a friend, trying to understand what they need, and then trying to help and serve. Each child will practice this in a small way during snack time. They will come alongside another child like a friend and get to know and understand their likes and dislikes, and then help them by serving them a snack.

Repeated Ideas for Lesson 3 "I Am Compassionate":
- Compassion is coming alongside someone who is suffering or struggling like a friend, trying to understand, and trying to help.
- God is compassionate. God comes alongside us, tries to understand, and helps us.
- We need to look at others through God's eyes of compassion.

Introductory Statement: Compassion is coming alongside someone as a friend, understanding them, and helping them. We're going to practice that during snack time! You will get to come alongside someone like a friend, try to understand what they need and want at snack time, and then you'll help them by serving them!

Instructions:
- During the snack time, each child will be put with a partner. They will serve their partner the snack.
- First, they will need to come alongside their partner, like a friend, and get to know what they like and don't like (as far as the snack). This can be as simple as asking them what they would like from the options, but it's still practicing asking people what they need and want.
- Then they will go up to the food table with all the options and make a plate for their partner, based on their partner's needs and wants, and then serve their partner.
- One partner will go first with serving, and then they'll switch.
- After everyone is served, you as a leader can help prompt them to talk to their partners (or those around them) about what they like and dislike (for example, "Share with your partner your favorite kind of ice cream" or "Share with your partner your favorite pet" or "Share with your partner your least favorite vegetable" or "Share with your partner your favorite church song", etc.).

Living God's Dream

Summary Statement (summarize main idea & connect back to the theme):
Remember, compassion is coming alongside someone like a friend, and trying to understand what they need, and then trying to help. You practiced that today! You came alongside your partner, you tried to understand what they wanted and needed for their snack, and then you helped them by going to get their snack for them and serving them! We can do this in lots of different ways, at home and in all kinds of places. We just have to get to know people and pay attention to what they might need, then try to help!

Serve/Do 3 | Make Meals

Supplies:
Check with your local soup kitchen about what they might need, but often they need plain sandwiches with bread, meat, cheese, and no condiments.

- Bread (2 slices per sandwich for as many sandwiches as are needed)
- Cheese (1 slice per sandwich)
- Deli-sliced lunch meat (3-4 slices per sandwich)
- Gloves
- Zip-closed plastic baggies

Overview for Leader: This activity activates compassion and puts it to work. When we understand what people need, compassion means that we try to help. This is a practical way for children to act on their compassion and try to help.

Repeated Ideas for Lesson 3 "I Am Compassionate":
- Compassion is coming alongside someone who is suffering or struggling like a friend, trying to understand, and trying to help.
- God is compassionate. God comes alongside us, tries to understand, and helps us.
- We need to look at others through God's eyes of compassion.

Introductory Statement: Compassion is coming alongside someone as a friend, understanding them, and helping them. There are many people in this world, even around us, who are hungry. We can understand what it's like to be hungry because we've all been hungry before. What do you need when YOU are hungry? Food? That's usually what I need! So, when we know that there are hungry people in our community, compassion means coming alongside them like a friend, understanding what they need (food), and trying to help. So today, we are going to help the hungry in our community by making them sandwiches, and we will drop them off at the soup kitchen where those who are hungry can get them!

Instructions:
- In preparation, set out bread, cheese, and meat in the middle of the table, so children can reach them.
- Gather the children away from the supplies to begin with for instructions.

Living God's Dream

- Remind the children about the definition of compassion: it is coming alongside someone as a friend, understanding them and what they need, and trying to help. Explain that this is a way we ACT on our compassion. We know that some people in our world don't have enough food and go hungry. If we are treating them as friends, we will see that they need food, and we will try to help take care of that need. Compassion and seeing people through God's eyes cause us to DO SOMETHING. So, we're going to do something today.
- Explain how to make the sandwiches, the quantities needed, how to put them in the baggies, and where to put them when they are finished.
- Explain what they will do, and what adults will help with (this will depend on their age).
- Explain health and safety practices: wearing gloves, not touching their mouth, nose, or face, mask-wearing as is necessary, etc.
- Give them time to make all the sandwiches you have using the supplies you have.
- As you are making sandwiches, talk with the children about times when they've been hungry, what it is like when someone has met their needs (needs may often be met by their caregivers, but also from other sources), what they hope and pray for the people who receive this food, etc.

LEADER TIP: in these imaginings, be careful of narratives that push stereotypes, like all hungry people are homeless or don't have jobs or things like that. This may happen just because of the messages floating around in society. You can tell stories about those you know, for whom a meal has been a blessing, like if you have brought meals to someone who was caring for a sick parent, or someone who had a family member die. If members of the recipient soup kitchen can be present to tell age-appropriate stories about those they serve, that might also help.

Summary Statement (summarize main idea of activity & connect to the theme):
You have just activated your compassion! Compassion is when we act as friends and neighbors to others, when we try to understand what they need, and try to help, and today, you had compassion, and you helped!

Let's say a prayer to bless this food and those who receive it. I wonder what are some things we can pray for those who are going to eat these sandwiches? (Listen to some answers.)

Say a prayer asking that this food would be healthy nourishment for the bodies of those who eat it, and that it would also nourish their souls, and let them know they are loved and worthy of care because they are made in God's image. Pray that we would see those around us with God's eyes of compassion, and that God would guide us in knowing how to help others.

Resources 3

For more resources on books about the immigrant and refugee experience, please visit the Resource section of the Diocese of Atlanta website (go to Resources>Education and Formation>Dismantling Racism Curriculum Resources).

Lesson/Day 4: I Am Resistant

- Theme: Resistance
- Main Idea: Stand firm and don't go along with unfairness
- Explanation/Teaching Approach: Society is set up so we will just go along with the way things are, but when we see that something is unfair, we have to stand firm to avoid being swept away with it (like a river current). We will be prompted to just move along with the current and go with the flow, but we have to actively try not to participate in that "current" when we see things that are not fair. We can't go along with it. We have to stand up, stand against, stand firm, and not be swept away.

Objectives:
- To understand what resistance is (not going along with something, standing firm against something, in this case, unfairness)
- To value resisting unfairness by engaging the idea of protest and other ways of resisting
- To practice resistance through making protest signs and writing letters

Elements:
1. Bible Story: Daniel. Both when he refuses to go along with the diet, but instead eats veggies and water, and when he refuses to stop praying, even though the consequence was the lion's den.
   a. Set up two picnic areas: one of good-tasting but bad-for-you food, and one with healthy veggies and fruit to help drive the first Daniel story home.
   b. Talk about ways we have to stand apart/be different/stick out to do the right thing.
2. Story Books:
   a. *This is Your Time* by Ruby Bridges
   b. *The Youngest Marcher* by Cynthia Levinson
   c. *That's Not My Name!* by Anoosha Syed
3. Personal Story: Story of resistance, not participating in unfairness, or protesting
   a. Dr. Catherine Meeks' story about the Doctor's Office waiting room
4. Art: Protest signs
   a. One silly thing you want to protest
   b. One problem in the world that you want fixed

Living God's Dream

5. Music: "Not Be Shaken" by Norm Strauss and "We Shall Not be Moved"
6. Play/Activity: "This Game is Very Fun," where you do silly things, but you have to resist laughing
7. Snack: Lion graham cracker head
8. Serve/Do:
    a. Hold protest signs they made up at the road of the church
    b. Join a march
    c. Letter writing campaign

Introduction to Lesson and Theme

Theme: Resistance
Main Idea: Stand firm and don't go along with unfairness

Upfront Illustration: Wind Resistance
- Supplies: light-weight items (like paper, feathers, leaves) and some anchoring items (like rocks and tape)
- Get a giant strong fan and some light-weight items (like feathers, paper, leaves). Place the items in front of the fan and ask the children what they think will happen if you turn it on. Then turn it on.
- Ask a few volunteers to come up and use the other items (like rocks and tape) to help make it so the light-weight items can resist being blown away. When they're ready, turn the fan on again and see what happens.
- You could also use a video of a sky-diving wind tunnel or of someone tubing down a river (particularly what happens when someone puts their feet up vs. when they put their feet down).

Introduce the Main Ideas (say something like):
Society is set up so we will just go along with the way things are, but when we see that something is unfair, we have to stand firm to avoid being swept away with it (like a river or air current). We will be prompted to just move along with the current and go with the flow, but we have to actively try not to participate in that "current" when we see things are not fair. We can't go along with it. We have to stand up, stand against, stand firm, and not be swept away.

In our first lesson, we learned that God made every single human being in God's image, which means there is goodness in each person that points us to God. We learned that humanity is diverse, that every single person is different on purpose, and that is how we get a more complete view of what God is like. Like a puzzle, each person is a piece of the picture, showing us what God is like, showing us God's goodness. We learned that God's dream is for us to see beauty in our differences and to love each person as God loves each person. We are all beloved.

In our second lesson, we learned that we often mess up God's dream for us to love each other and to be blessed by our differences. Instead of loving the things that make us different and unique, humans often view differences as dangerous or evil, and use differences as an excuse to exclude others, separate from each other, or treat others unfairly. We make a mess when

Living God's Dream

we do this. And it takes a lot of courage to face the messes and to try to work on them to make them better.

In our third lesson, we learned that one way that helps make the mess better is to see everyone through God's eyes of compassion, which means we come alongside someone who is struggling or is going through hardship, and we try to understand them, and we try to help. Seeing everyone through God's eyes of compassion can help heal the world's mess.

Today, we're going to learn another way that we can help work on the messes and bring God's dream of loving each other to earth: resistance. When you resist something, you don't participate in it. Think about it like a river or a strong wind with a fast, swift current. If you've ever been tubing in a river, you know if you put your feet up, the current just sweeps you along. But if you plant your feet and stand your ground, you can resist the current and keep it from sweeping you along. The messy world is set up to keep the unfairness going. The unfairness we learned about is like the river, which just keeps going. We have to resist it; we have to plant our feet and stand firm against that current. We have to resist going along with unfairness. So, when we see someone being made fun of, or not being treated with kindness or respect, or being treated badly just because they are different, we have to *resist*! We can't go along with that.

And that's a way that we can help make the world better, more like God intended. Resist!

Repeated Ideas:
- Resistance means to stand firm against something, and for the purpose of these lessons, it means to not participate in unfairness or unkindness, to stand firm against those things.
- Resisting unfairness is a way to help the world become more fair and good, like God intended.

Bible Story 4 | Daniel & Resistance

Part 1 - Choosing the Right Food

Scripture Reference: Daniel 1

In the third year of the reign of Jehoiakim king of Judah, Nebuchadnezzar king of Babylon came to Jerusalem and besieged it. ² *And the Lord delivered Jehoiakim king of Judah into his hand, along with some of the articles from the temple of God. These he carried off to the temple of his god in Babylonia[a] and put in the treasure house of his god.*

³ *Then the king ordered Ashpenaz, chief of his court officials, to bring into the king's service some of the Israelites from the royal family and the nobility…*

⁶ *Among those who were chosen were some from Judah: Daniel, Hananiah, Mishael and Azariah.* ⁷ *The chief official gave them new names: to Daniel, the name Belteshazzar; to Hananiah, Shadrach; to Mishael, Meshach; and to Azariah, Abednego.*

⁸ *But Daniel resolved not to defile himself with the royal food and wine, and he asked the chief official for permission not to defile himself this way.* ⁹ *Now God had caused the official to show favor and compassion to Daniel,* ¹⁰ *but the official told Daniel, "I am afraid of my lord the king, who has assigned your[c] food and drink. Why should he see you looking worse than the other young men your age? The king would then have my head because of you."*

¹¹ *Daniel then said to the guard whom the chief official had appointed over Daniel, Hananiah, Mishael and Azariah,* ¹² *"Please test your servants for ten days: Give us nothing but vegetables to eat and water to drink.* ¹³ *Then compare our appearance with that of the young men who eat the royal food, and treat your servants in accordance with what you see."* ¹⁴ *So he agreed to this and tested them for ten days.*

¹⁵ *At the end of the ten days they looked healthier and better nourished than any of the young men who ate the royal food.* ¹⁶ *So the guard took away their choice food and the wine they were to drink and gave them vegetables instead.*

Supplies/Setup:

You will need two blankets and a variety of foods to set up two separate picnic areas. One picnic area, the larger of the two, should have all sorts of unhealthy food and drink that children love to eat: chips, candy, sugary baked goods, soda, etc. The other, smaller picnic area should only have water and fresh vegetables.

Overview for Leader: This illustration is designed to give the children a feel for what it would have been like for Daniel to resist what was expected of him and stand out from the crowd in order to obey God. Before telling the story of Daniel being recruited into the king's service, you will invite the children to take a seat at one of two picnics: one of water and vegetables, and the other of rich, sweet, indulgent foods. There may be a few kids that choose the water and vegetables before hearing the story, but even those kids will likely express some feelings of awkwardness at sitting all alone during the story while others sat together with friends. In the same way, even though Daniel knew he was choosing what was right, doing so required him to resist the temptation to take the easier route.

Repeated Ideas for Lesson 4 "I Am Resistant":
- Resistance means to stand firm against something, and for the purpose of these lessons, it means to not participate in unfairness or unkindness, to stand firm against those things.
- Resisting unfairness is a way to help the world become more fair and good, like God intended.

Storytelling Technique: Participate in the story
- As the children arrive, ask them to take a seat around the picnic area that they would like to eat from, but not to eat just yet. It is very likely that they will all sit around the first picnic area that has unhealthy food, and that is okay!
- Now read through or summarize the story told in Daniel 1.
  - King Nebuchadnezzar wanted strong young men to work for him and had them train for three years to get ready, which included eating rich, fancy, and sometimes unhealthy food.
  - Daniel was one of the young men that was recruited to be in the King's service.
  - Daniel was an Israelite and loved God. God had asked Daniel to not eat the unhealthy food and Daniel wanted to remain loyal to God, so he refused to eat it.
  - The king's officials were angry about that but agreed to let him eat only vegetables and drink water for ten days. If after ten days Daniel still looked healthy, then they wouldn't make him eat the king's food.
  - At the end of the ten days, Daniel looked even healthier than the others and was allowed to still be in the king's service and still remain loyal to God!
- Take some time to discuss the main points from the story and wonder about how their current picnic situation may help us understand what it would have been like for Daniel.
  - I wonder where Daniel would sit if he was invited to our picnic. I wonder if he had to sit alone. Would it be hard for him to sit there? I wonder if Daniel ever wanted to give up.
  - I wonder why God asked Daniel to not eat the king's food. I wonder if he wished he could eat it.

- You may also want to invite a child to sit alone at the healthier picnic for a while and share what that experience was like.

"Wondering" Questions:

I wonder if you've ever had to resist doing something that everyone else was doing? I wonder what that felt like? I wonder how you managed to do that or what kept you strong? I wonder what it would have felt like for Daniel to resist eating the delicious food? I wonder how he managed to resist? I wonder if you think you could have done that if you were in his position?

Summary Statement (summarize main idea & connect back to theme):

Today's Bible story tells us about how Daniel had to do something differently from those around him because he knew that's what God wanted him to do. Daniel only ate the food that God told him to, even though there was a lot of pressure to eat the rich and fancy food. He didn't refuse to eat the other food because it was bad for him, but because God asked him not to. The other food would have been yummy, but Daniel knew he'd rather stand firm and do what he promised to God. In the same way, there are times in our lives when God asks us to do things that no one else around us is doing, which often makes the decision to do it even harder! Following God and resisting the urge to follow the crowd often means that we will have to stand firm against things that are unfair and unkind. But when we do those things, when we stand firm and resist, we are helping make the world become a more fair and better place, just as God intends.

Part 2 - Prayer

Scripture Reference: Daniel 6

³ Now Daniel so distinguished himself among the administrators and the satraps by his exceptional qualities that the king planned to set him over the whole kingdom. ⁴ At this, the administrators and the satraps tried to find grounds for charges against Daniel in his conduct of government affairs, but they were unable to do so. They could find no corruption in him, because he was trustworthy and neither corrupt nor negligent. ⁵ Finally these men said, "We will never find any basis for charges against this man Daniel unless it has something to do with the law of his God."

⁶ So these administrators and satraps went as a group to the king and said: "May King Darius live forever! ⁷ The royal administrators, prefects, satraps, advisers and governors have all agreed that the king should issue an edict and enforce the decree that anyone who prays to any god or human being during the next thirty days, except to you, Your Majesty, shall be thrown into the lions' den. ⁸ Now, Your Majesty, issue the decree and put it in writing so that it cannot be altered—in accordance with the law of the Medes and Persians, which cannot be repealed." ⁹ So King Darius put the decree in writing.

¹⁰ Now when Daniel learned that the decree had been published, he went home to his upstairs room where the windows opened toward Jerusalem. Three times a day he got down on his knees and prayed, giving thanks to his God, just as he had done before....

¹⁶ So the king gave the order, and they brought Daniel and threw him into the lions' den. The king said to Daniel, "May your God, whom you serve continually, rescue you!"

¹⁷ A stone was brought and placed over the mouth of the den, and the king sealed it with his own signet ring and with the rings of his nobles, so that Daniel's situation might not be changed...

¹⁹ At the first light of dawn, the king got up and hurried to the lions' den. ²⁰ When he came near the den, he called to Daniel in an anguished voice, "Daniel, servant of the living God, has your God, whom you serve continually, been able to rescue you from the lions?"

²¹ Daniel answered, "May the king live forever! ²² My God sent his angel, and he shut the mouths of the lions. They have not hurt me, because I was found innocent in his sight. Nor have I ever done any wrong before you, Your Majesty."

Supplies/Setup: Something to make a lion's den. It can be a bunch of cardboard boxes.

Overview for Leader: This story is another example of how Daniel resisted being assimilated into the dominant culture. He resisted unfairness and continued to do what God asked him to do, even though he faced consequences. Consequences might be scary, but we can remind students that we are brave, and that God is with us, so we can do hard things. When acting this out, especially the lions attacking (but not touching) Daniel, pull back if any child is afraid. This is challenge by choice, and if they choose to participate, that's great, but if at any point it feels too scary and they don't want to continue, be sure to honor that and do not shame them for not completing the activity. They are invited to participate however they want to, with no strings attached.

Repeated Ideas for Lesson 4 "I Am Resistant":
- Resistance means to stand firm against something, and for the purpose of these lessons, it means to not participate in unfairness or unkindness, to stand firm against those things.
- Resisting unfairness is a way to help the world become more fair and better, like God intended.

Storytelling Technique: Participating in the story
- Summarize the main points of the story about Daniel in the Lion's Den. You might choose to read this story out of a Children's Bible, and then summarize.
  - Daniel was an official in the Babylonian kingdom.
  - Everyone else in Babylon believed the king was better than everyone else. Daniel believed that every single person was created in God's image and was equal, and the only one greater than everyone else was God. Daniel would only worship God and refused to worship the king or any other human being. He would not treat some people better than other people.
  - Because Daniel treated everyone fairly and was trustworthy and good, the king wanted to reward him. That made the other officials jealous. When the other officials saw that Daniel only worshipped God, they thought that might be a way to trap him. So, they went to the king and asked the king to make it a law that everyone had to worship the king. They knew Daniel wouldn't go along with it. They did it on purpose to try to get him in trouble.
  - Daniel resisted this law because he knew that human beings were equal; he knew only God deserved worship, and it's not right to treat some people better than others. So, he did not worship the king and instead continued worshipping God. When the officials caught him doing this, he was thrown into the Lion's Den, as the law required.
  - God sent an angel to protect Daniel in the Lion's Den. No lion could touch him!
- The children can take turns acting out resisting the decree, praying, and being in the lions' den. This is all "challenge by choice," so children volunteer to participate and only need to participate as much as they feel comfortable doing so.
  - All the children who want to can pretend to pray to the king.

- The child pretending to be Daniel can practice resisting, saying something like, "I will only worship God" or "I will not treat some people better than others" or "I will keep praying to God."
- The child will kneel to pray.
- Then help that child into the Lion's Den area. Other children can pretend to be lions and growl and prowl around, but they CANNOT TOUCH "Daniel." Another child can be an Angel and stand between Daniel and the Lions. No one can touch anyone else.
- Children can take turns being the different roles. Younger children may want to do this many times. Older children may only want to do it once or a few times.

"Wondering" Questions:

I wonder if you've ever had to resist doing something that everyone else was doing? I wonder what Daniel might have felt like to be the only one doing something different? I wonder what it would have felt like to stand up against something you knew was wrong and not participate in it? I wonder what it was like to be in the Lion's Den? Being scared by trying to trust that God would take care of you? I wonder if you've ever been in Daniel's position and had to resist doing something you thought was unfair? I wonder what that was like?

Summary Statement (summarize main idea & connect back to theme):

Resistance means to stand firm against something, and for the purpose of these lessons, it means to not participate in unfairness or unkindness, to stand firm against those things. Daniel knew that only God should be worshipped, and that some human beings, like the king, shouldn't be treated better than everyone else. He knew it was not right to treat some people like they were God, like they were better. Resisting unfairness is a way to help the world become more fair and better, like God intended.

Story Book 4

Option 1: *This is Your Time* by Ruby Bridges (elementary)

Overview for Leader: In this book, Ruby Bridges shares about what it was like to be the first black child to go to an all-white school, thus beginning the process of desegregating public schools. Ruby had so many mixed feelings during that time, but she and her family were able to continue to stand for what was right despite the challenges and intimidation. She also shares about how she has seen things change over the years and how there is so much work to do, but that there is hope in how children see each other.

Repeated Ideas for Lesson 4 "I Am Resistant":
- Resistance means to stand firm against something, and for the purpose of these lessons, it means to not participate in unfairness or unkindness, to stand firm against those things.
- Resisting unfairness is a way to help the world become better and more fair, like God intended.

Introductory Statement: Today we have been talking about resisting things that we know to be unfair and are not what God would want. There are many things in our nation's history that have made God sad, and brave people have had to resist in order to create change. Sometimes those people have been children! This is a story of a girl named Ruby Bridges, who was the first black child to go to school with white children. Ruby went to school in 1960 when she was only six years old, and before that, our nation's schools were separated into schools for white children and schools for children of color. This was known as segregation. Ruby was allowed to be at the new school, but some people didn't want her there and were unkind and tried to convince her to not go. But, as you will learn, Ruby was brave and resisted the people who tried to keep her from going where she deserved to be.

Read the Story: *This is Your Time* by Ruby Bridges, Delacorte Press, 2020

"Wondering" Questions:
- I wonder what it felt like to be Ruby Bridges in 1960. I wonder what her parents said to her when they sent her to school so that she would be brave. I wonder what it felt like to have all those adults yelling at her as she walked into school? I wonder if she wanted to play with the other children. I wonder if her teacher, Barbara Henry, and her friends helped her be brave.

- I wonder what it was like for the white children who went to school with Ruby. I wonder what their parents told them about Ruby. I wonder if they wanted to play with Ruby. Were they curious about her?
- I wonder what I would have done if I went to school with Ruby. Would I have wanted to be her friend? Would I have invited her to my birthday party? Would she have invited me to her birthday party?
- I wonder what I would have done if I saw someone being mean to Ruby. What do I do now when I see someone being unkind? How have I stood up for people when they are being treated poorly?
- I wonder how school is different now than when Ruby was in school? Have children changed? Have their parents changed? Are we sometimes still unkind to each other?

Summary Statement (summarize main idea of story & connect back to theme):
Throughout the Bible, God gives us so many examples of people who were able to do what God asked of them and resist doing the things that would make God sad. Ruby's story doesn't appear in the Bible, but it is in much more recent history! When she was just a little girl, she was able to be strong and listen to the truth of God, and not the voices from people who were being hateful. She made such a huge difference in the story of our country, and she was only six years old. Her story shows us that, no matter what our age, God gives us all the ability to stand up for what is right. We don't have to wait on adults to do the work. We can all help!

Option 2: *The Youngest Marcher* (elementary)

Overview for Leader: This is the true story of a young child who was a civil rights activist fighting for an end to segregation. The story helps share the experiences of a child during segregation, how she felt, and how she wanted to participate in stopping the unfairness. During the Civil Rights movement, students, young adults and even children, participated in sit-ins and marches, and were arrested en masse, filling the jails so their parents wouldn't be penalized for missing work, and then when other adults protested, there was no room in the jails.

Repeated Ideas for Lesson 4 "I Am Resistant":
- Resistance means to stand firm against something, and for the purpose of these lessons, it means to not participate in unfairness or unkindness, to stand firm against those things.
- Resisting unfairness is a way to help the world become better and more fair, like God intended.

Introductory Statement:
When we see injustice or unfairness, we must resist it. We can't go along with it. Even children can resist. In fact, throughout our history, we see that children can make a difference! This is a story of resistance. Audrey saw unfairness and would not go along with it. She protested and resisted the unfairness of segregation. And you know what? It made a difference.

Read the Story: *The Youngest Marcher: The Story of Aubrey Faye Hendricks, A Young Civil Rights Activist* by Cynthia Levinson, illustrated by Vanessa Brantley-Newton, Atheneum Books for Young Readers, 2017

"Wondering" Questions:
- I wonder what it would be like to see and experience the unfairness Audrey saw and experienced? I wonder what I would have done or wanted to do when I saw that kind of unfairness?
- I wonder what you think of what Audrey decided to do? I wonder how it would feel to go to jail for not going along with unjust laws?
- I wonder where you saw hardship or struggle or unfairness in the story? I wonder where you saw kindness and hope and goodness in the story?
- I wonder how you see that things are different today than they were then?
- I wonder how we can keep resisting unfairness? I wonder if we do keep resisting unfairness how the world will be better and what that will look like?

Summary Statement (summarize main idea of story & connect back to theme):
When we see unfairness, that goes against God's dream, and God calls us to do something about it—to not just go along with it, but to resist it. Sometimes that is hard work, sometimes even harder than we think it will be. But remember, God is always with us to help us do the work of making God's dream for us a reality! And it does make a difference!

Option 3: *That's Not My Name!* (Pre-K/K and up)

Overview for Leader: This is the story of a young child's first day at school, when her classmates can't pronounce her name correctly. It is about how she is tempted to go along with their mispronunciations so as not to make waves, but how she finds the courage to resist that unfair treatment (even if it was well-intentioned) and stand up for herself. Even insisting that her classmates get her name right is a small act of resistance to the messages that she should make it easier for her classmates by allowing them to call her something that isn't her name, or that her name is perhaps not worth the effort, or that by calling her something else, her name is somehow "less than." It's a small act of resistance that can have a big impact and may resonate more with younger children.

Repeated Ideas for Lesson 4 "I Am Resistant":
- Resistance means to stand firm against something, and for the purpose of these lessons, it means to not participate in unfairness or unkindness, to stand firm against those things.
- Resisting unfairness is a way to help the world become better and more fair, like God intended.

Introductory Statement:
I wonder if someone has ever gotten your name wrong before? Or maybe called you a nickname you didn't like? I wonder if you remember how that feels? When we call someone by the name they want to be called, we are honoring something about who they are. The author of this story is Anoosha Syed, and she grew up in Canada, where a lot of people got her name wrong. Perhaps it made her feel like there was something wrong with her name, or even that there was something wrong with her, so she wrote this book because she didn't want children to feel like that. When we don't take the time to learn how to say someone's name, it is not treating them with fairness or kindness, and we need to resist that. If someone is not calling you by your name, you can resist that by explaining "That's Not My Name." And if you see that others are not calling someone else by their name, you also can resist that unfairness by saying, "That's not their name," and taking the time to say it correctly.

Read the Story: *That's Not My Name!* by Anoosha Syed, Viking Books for Young Readers, 2022

"Wondering" Questions:
- I wonder if you've ever had the experience of someone saying your name wrong? Maybe it was not intentional, or maybe it was on purpose (like sometimes kids give each other nicknames they don't like)? I wonder what that felt like?
- Mirha seems to like her name and wants others to say it correctly. I wonder why Mirha didn't say anything at first when people got her name wrong?
- After a day of being called the wrong name, it seems like Mirha doesn't like her name as much. I wonder why Mirha wanted to change her name?
- I wonder what helped her understand her name was special and was worth saying correctly?
- I wonder how she was feeling when she was going to tell Hayden to pronounce her name correctly? I wonder if she was worried about how he would react?
- I wonder about how she is feeling when people decide to say her name correctly? I wonder how she feels learning about other people's names and why they were named what they were?
- I wonder if you know about your name and why you were named what you were? I wonder what you like about your name?

Summary Statement (summarize main idea of story & connect back to theme):
When someone doesn't say another person's name correctly, they might have good intentions. They might not mean to hurt someone's feelings. Maybe they are just trying to make it easier, because it feels hard or awkward and takes a lot of practice to say someone's name when it isn't familiar. They might not mean to be unkind or unfair. But the impact of not saying someone's name correctly is that it *does* hurt their feelings, and it sends the message that their name is not important—maybe even that *they* are not important. We don't want to do that! We know that everyone is important and loved by God! We want to make sure we are resisting that idea that someone's name isn't important. Even just taking the time to learn to say someone's name right is a way to resist unfairness and unkindness. It might seem small, but it is a big deal to the person to hear their name said correctly, and it helps send the message that every person is important!

Personal Story | Resistance by Dr. Catherine Meeks

Overview for Leader:
Dr. Catherine Meeks is the founder of the Absalom Jones Center for Racial Healing, which is a ministry of the Diocese of Atlanta in collaboration with the Presiding Bishop's office; she has been doing the work of dismantling racism for most of her life. Dr. Meeks tells the story of a time she resisted the message of being "less than." This is a personal story that demonstrates what resistance might look like in real life.

Repeated Ideas for Lesson 4 "I Am Resistant":
- Resistance means to stand firm against something, and for the purpose of these lessons, it means to not participate in unfairness or unkindness, to stand firm against those things.
- Resisting unfairness is a way to help the world become better and more fair, like God intended.

Introductory Statement:
I wonder what it means to resist unfairness in real, everyday life? We're going to hear a story about what it can look like to resist unfairness. We're going to hear from Dr. Catherine Meeks. Dr. Meeks is the founder of the Absalom Jones Center for Racial Healing, and she has been trying to resist unfairness, particularly racism, which is where people are treated unfairly because of their race, for most of her life. She's going to tell the story of one of the first times she remembers resisting the message society was telling her, that she was "less than" other people because she was Black. She resisted that message. And she has continued to resist it. Here's a story about how she resists.

Show video:
Videos can be found at the Diocese of Atlanta website under Resources>Education & Formation Resources, then click on the Dismantling Racism Curriculum Resources.
You can also invite someone from your context to share a personal story about a time when they resisted unfairness and did not go along with it.

Summary Statement (summarize main idea of story & connect back to theme):
Not sitting down might seem like a small thing, but for Dr. Meeks, it was an act of resistance that meant something big and important. It was saying that she would not go along with

Living God's Dream

the unfair message about her not having a place in society, about her being considered as "less than" other people. Acts of resistance can be big or small. We need to continue to resist unfairness in big and small ways. We cannot go along with it when other people, who are loved by God and created in God's image, are treated unfairly.

Art 4 | Protest Signs

Supplies:
Thick Poster Board or Cardboard
Markers
Glue or Masking Tape
Paint Sticks (Optional)
Stencils (Optional)

Overview for Leader: The children have heard the story of Daniel and the modern stories of people taking a stand when they feel someone has not treated them fairly, or like Daniel, someone wanting them to do something that was not right. You are going to make two signs. The first will be a fun sign (think of the Chick Fil A signs of cows holding signs Eat Mor Chiken). The second sign will be the protest sign. Talk about some things that they should stand up for/resist. These will be the things they write on their signs. You can remind them of the stories they have heard. You can also pull some examples from Google Images or iStock. If you use the internet for examples, *please search in advance*.

Repeated Ideas for Lesson 4 "I Am Resistant":
- Resistance means to stand firm against something, and for the purpose of these lessons, it means to not participate in unfairness or unkindness, to stand firm against those things.
- Resisting unfairness is a way to help the world become better and more fair, like God intended.

Introductory Statement:
Words are powerful and speaking is one way we can express how we feel, but we want to show other ways that people have stood up for injustice. Signs are excellent because they are something that people can see. When they read our signs, they may not realize they have joined our stand.

Instructions:
- Write with a pencil on the poster board what you would like the sign to say.
- Trace over the letters with the markers.
- If using paint sticks, tape or glue on the back of the sign.
- Remember, paint sticks are optional. Signs can be handheld as well.

Summary Statement (summarize main idea of art & connect back to the theme):
There are times when people are not treated fairly. God commanded us to not only love God but to also love our neighbor. So, when we see or hear about someone being mistreated, there are many ways that we can do something about it. We can pray for them, we can sign petitions, and we can start or join in the protest. Adults can also help us think of other ways.

Music 4

Songs: "Not Be Shaken" and "We Shall Not Be Moved"

<u>Song #1</u>: "Not Be Shaken" by Norm Strauss, from Mercy/Vineyard Publishing, 1997. This song is covered under CCLI licensing.

Overivew for Leader: The song is based on words of many different Psalms, including Psalm 16, 20, 62, and more.

Repeated Ideas for Lesson 4 "I Am Resistant":
- Resistance means to stand firm against something, and for the purpose of these lessons, it means to not participate in unfairness or unkindness, to stand firm against those things.
- Resisting unfairness is a way to help the world become better and more fair,, like God intended.

Introductory Statement to Singing the Song: The words of this song are based on several passages from the Bible, mostly Psalms, which were written to be sung. It talks about how sometimes we have to stand firm, and when we stand firm and do what God wants us to do, it's like standing on a firm rock...when everything else is crumbling, we won't, because we've chosen to stand with God, and do what God wants. We stand firm, and we can resist the unfairness, and God helps us. We will not be shaken, and we won't be moved. We stand firm.

Special Instructions/Motions:
You can always invite children to consider the words, and to help create motions to the song.

Summary Statement (summarize main idea & connect back to the theme):
Resistance means we stand against unfairness, and we don't go along with it. That is what God asks us to do, and so God will be with us to help us do that. When we resist unfairness, it's like we are standing on a firm rock that can't be shaken or moved. And when we resist, it helps the world become a more fair and just place.

Living God's Dream

Song #2: "We Shall Not Be Moved"

Overview for Leader: This is a spiritual, a hymn, and a protest song sung during the Civil Rights movement, that may have even originated before emancipation from slavery. For more resources about the history of this song, visit the resource section of the Diocese of Atlanta website. This song was sung during the Civil Rights movement of the 50s and 60s, and even before that during the Labor movement of the 30s and 40s. Some scholars believe it may even have originated as an African American spiritual before Emancipation. It is about resistance. It is based on Scripture from Jeremiah and Psalm 1:

- *"But blessed is the one who trusts in the Lord, whose confidence is in him. They will be like a tree planted by the water that sends out its roots by the stream. It does not fear when heat comes; its leaves are always green. It has no worries in a year of drought and never fails to bear fruit." —Jeremiah 17:7-8*
- *That person is like a tree planted by streams of water, which yields its fruit in season and whose leaf does not wither—whatever they do prospers. —Psalm 1:3*

Repeated Ideas for Lesson 4 "I Am Resistant":
- Resistance means to stand firm against something, and for the purpose of these lessons, it means to not participate in unfairness or unkindness, to stand firm against those things.
- Resisting unfairness is a way to help the world become better and more fair,, like God intended.

Introductory Statement to Singing the Song: We read about some of the children who protested unfairness, especially during the Civil Rights Movement. Remember the Civil Rights Movement was when people protested the unjust segregation laws that separated black people and white people and left black people out. Protesting is a form of resisting, of not going along with unfairness. During some of the protests, protestors would sing this song.

Special Instructions/Motions/Lyrics:
You can search on the internet for original audio recordings of this song being sung by protestors.

Summary Statement (summarize main idea & connect back to the theme):
Resistance means standing firm against unfairness, and it is what God wants us to do, so when we do it, we know that God will be with us to help us. Resistance is one way we can help make the world more like God dreamed it to be!

Play/Activity 4

Option 1: "This Game is Very Fun"

Supplies: None needed, just the children.

Overview for Leader:
Walking the line between having fun and taking resistance seriously, this game may need some context. While we want to have fun, we also want to recognize that resistance has not always been fun for those who resist, and we don't want to make light of that, so it might be good to remind children about that when debriefing. In the game, they are supposed to resist laughing, and sometimes in life we are supposed to resist laughing at and making fun of others. However, this is just a game, and we don't want to shame children who might laugh as if they did the wrong thing. So, while this game is just for fun, and it's ok to laugh and to try not to laugh in games, in real life, God does call us to resist treating people unfairly, and sometimes that means not laughing.

Repeated Ideas for Lesson 4 "I Am Resistant":
- Resistance means to stand firm against something, and for the purpose of these lessons, it means to not participate in unfairness or unkindness, to stand firm against those things.
- Resisting unfairness is a way to help the world become better and more fair., like God intended.

Introductory Statement: Resistance means to stand firm against something, and today we've talked about how we have to stand firm against unfairness and not go along with it. One example might be making fun of someone. Maybe you're not even the one making fun of someone, but if you're going along with it, you're not resisting. It might be tempting to go along with this kind of unfairness because if you stand against the person who's making fun of someone else, they might turn on you next. Or maybe everyone else will think you're not fun or cool and leave you out. So, it's tempting to just go along with it (or even participate in it), but we've learned that going along with unfairness makes the world a mess, and God has this beautiful dream of everyone loving each other, but if we go along with unfairness, we'll miss out on experiencing that beautiful love! So, one way we can make God's dream real is to resist unfairness. If someone is getting made fun of, we need to stand firm against it. We have to not laugh, even when it seems like that's the thing to do. Sometimes we have to resist laughing at a joke that makes fun of someone else. In this game, we're going to try to resist laughing. This is just a game, so if you laugh, it's ok. But in real life, if we laugh at people or make fun of them, it can really do damage.

Instructions:
- Put the children in pairs.
- They will go through 3 rounds of this game with their partner and try not to laugh. If someone smiles or laughs during Round 1, then that person is out, and the other person wins, and goes on to find a new partner. If neither person smiles or laughs, then they go on to Round 2, and so on.
- Round 1: They will stand across from their partner, and with a straight face, no laughter or smiling, they have to say at the same time "This game is very fun" 5 times in a row.
- Round 2: They will stand across from their partner, and with a straight face, no laughter or smiling, and while jumping up and down, they have to say at the same time "This game is very fun" 5 times in a row.
- Round 3: They will stand across from their partner, and with a straight face, no laughter or smiling, and while jumping up and down, and while placing their hand on their partner's cheek, they have to say at the same time "This game is very fun" 5 times in a row.
- If they both can do three rounds without laughing or smiling, then they both win and can both find a new partner. Keep playing until there is only one winner.
- If you want the ones who laughed or smiled (and lost a round) to have the opportunity to keep playing just for fun, have them pair up with someone else who has lost a round. You might separate those who have not lost and are still "in" the game on one side of the room, and those who have laughed or smiled to another side of the room.
- Leaders can freely adapt some of the actions in these rounds to meet the needs and comfort levels of the children playing. The actions are intended to get sillier and sillier, so that it's hard to resist laughing.

Debrief/Discussion:
I wonder what it was like to try not to laugh? I wonder if there are times where it's good to laugh? I wonder if you can think of any times where it wouldn't be good to laugh?

Summary Statement (summarize main idea of activity & connect back to the theme): Sometimes it's appropriate to laugh at silly things, so it's ok if you laughed during this game. But sometimes it's not good to laugh, even though everyone else is doing it, because it's hurtful to someone else, and those are the times we have to resist, and we have to stand firm against unfairness, and we can't go along with it, even though it would be easy to. Resisting means standing firm against something, and one way we are called by God to resist is by resisting unfairness, standing firm against it, and not going along with it. We can't make the world a more fair and just place unless we resist unfairness.

Option 2: The Push Game

Supplies: No supplies needed, just the children

Overview for Leader:
This game illustrates physical resistance. They have to literally resist the force of someone pushing on them and try to stand firm and keep their balance. When using this as an analogy about how we have to resist the forces of unfairness that try to knock people over by treating them unkindly and unfairly, make sure to build careful and intentional bridges, especially for younger children, between the concrete (literally being pushed over) and the abstract (metaphorically resisting when people try to treat others unfairly).

Repeated Ideas for Lesson 4 "I Am Resistant":
- Resistance means to stand firm against something, and for the purpose of these lessons, it means to not participate in unfairness or unkindness, to stand firm against those things.
- Resisting unfairness is a way to help the world become better and more fair, like God intended.

Introductory Statement:
Resistance means to stand firm against something, and today we've talked about how we have to stand firm against unfairness and not go along with it. We've talked about how the world has lots of unfairness in it, and that unfairness just keeps going without any help, kind of like how a river just flows. We could be carried along with the river, or we could put our feet down, plant our feet firmly, and stand against the current. Then we wouldn't go along. Unfairness is like the river that just goes along, and we will go along with it unless we stand firm against it. In this game, you will need to stand firm and resist being pushed over.

Instructions:
- Put the children in pairs.
- Have them stand facing each other, arms' length apart (they can measure this by putting their arms on each other's shoulders, and making sure they are standing far enough away from each other so that their arms can be straight out in front of them, not bent).
- Once they are the correct distance, they will need to plant their feet in that spot, and their feet must be together, not apart.
- They need to hold their hands up, about shoulder height, but out to the side of their shoulders (not in front of their chest).

- The object of the game is to push the other person over, without moving from their spot, using only their hands and touching only their partner's hands.
- They will have to resist the force of their partner's pushing and try to keep their balance and their feet planted firmly.
- When one falls over, that person is out, and the winner goes on to find someone else who is still "in", who has not lost a round.
- Play until one person is left.
- Again, if you want to allow those who lost a round to play more, they can play others who have also lost a round just for fun.
- Leaders should modify games as needed for their group for safety, accessibility, and inclusion, and children should have options about how they choose to participate.

Debrief/Discussion:

I wonder if anyone would like to share a highlight of their experience during the game? Any interesting things that happened? I wonder what it was like for those of you who lost your balance? I wonder what it was like for those of you who didn't lose your balance…did you have any close calls where you almost lost your balance, and had to fight to keep standing steady?

Summary Statement (summarize main idea of the activity and connect back to theme): Unfairness is like a force that is trying to push us to go along with it. But we have to resist. We have to try to keep our feet planted firmly and not give in. Sometimes we may get pushed off balance, and it may be hard to resist, but we can always get back up again and keep on standing firm. If we want to change the world, we can't go along with unfairness. We have to resist it. We have to stand against it.

Snack 4 | Lion Graham Cracker Head

Supplies:
- Graham cracker sheets, broken in half
- Creamy peanut butter OR another sweet, spreadable (especially an option without nuts) to act as glue
- Stick pretzels
- Small, twisted pretzels
- Raisins OR some other small, sweet item to act as eyes
- Other snacks that might be fun to use for a lion face!
- Plates
- Plastic knives

Overview for Leader: Today's snack is a fun reminder of the lesson we had today about Daniel and the Lion's Den. Children will have a chance to create their own lion face snack and think about what it means to stand firm in their beliefs, even when it means facing a lion!

Repeated Ideas for Lesson 4 "I Am Resistant":
- Resistance means to stand firm against something, and for the purpose of these lessons, it means to not participate in unfairness or unkindness, to stand firm against those things.
- Resisting unfairness is a way to help the world become better and more fair, like God intended.

Introductory Statement: Earlier today we talked about lions and how Daniel chose to do what he knew to be right, even if that meant being thrown in a den of lions. Daniel prayed, trusted God, and was kept safe from the lions because he knew God was stronger than any lion! As a reminder of how Daniel resisted the temptation to fear the lion's den, we will make a snack that looks like a lion and DEVOUR it!

Instructions:
- Pass out plates, knives, and other supplies. If the graham crackers aren't already broken in half, you might want to help them with that part.
- Spread the peanut butter on the cracker to act as a glue for the other elements.
- Break the stick pretzels in half and place on the end of the cracker to act as a mane.
- Place a twisty pretzel in the center, upside down, to act as the lion's nose and mouth.
- Use two raisins for eyes.

- Before inviting the children to DEVOUR their snacks, ask them which elements of today's Bible story relate to the lion. The lions in the den? That we are sometimes called to be brave and not back down, just like Daniel did when he was threatened with the lion's den.
- How have they felt protected by God, like a lion cares for its cubs?
- Enjoy the snack!

Summary Statement (summarize main idea & connect back to the theme):
As you enjoy your lion snack, remember that God has called us to stand firm when we know something is right. Even when it is scary to do the right thing, we can trust that God is with us and will give us the strength to do what is kind and fair. With God, we can stand firm even against lions!

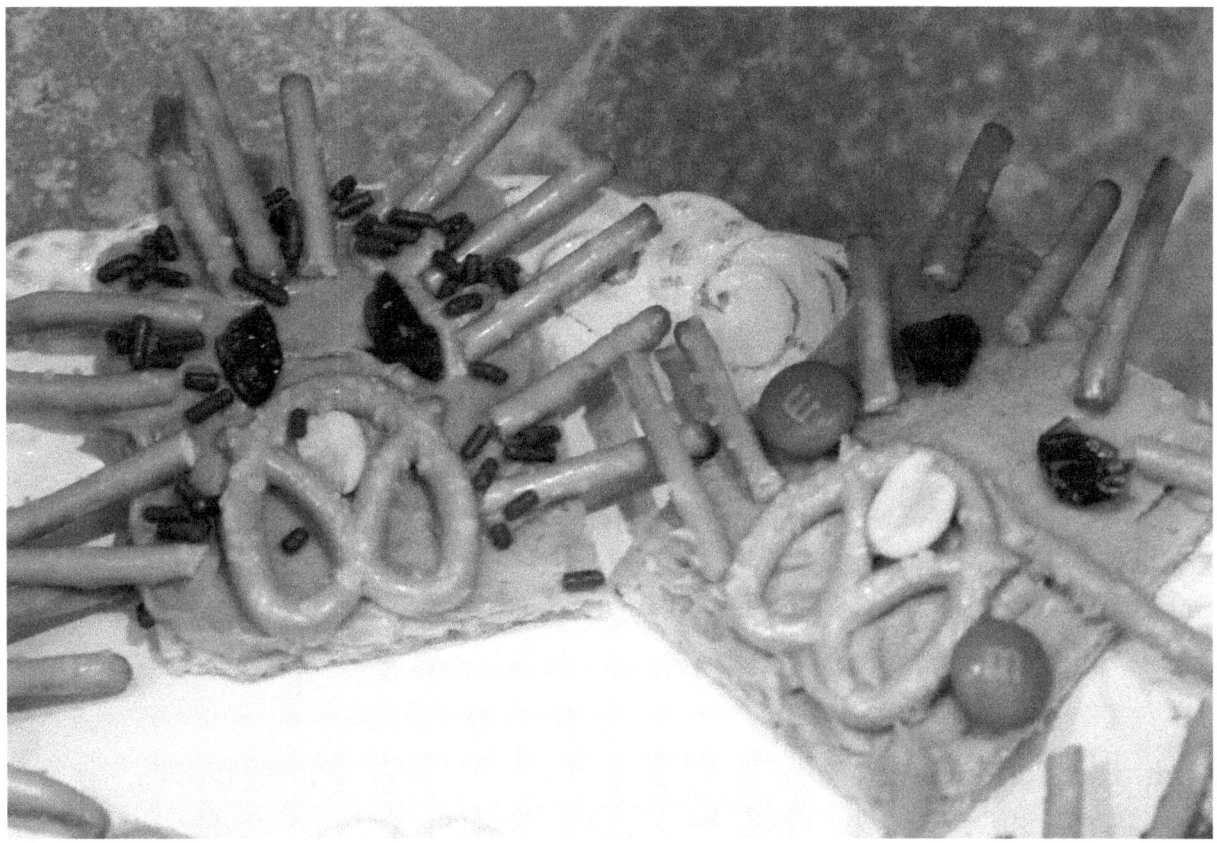

Serve/Do 4 | Protest

Option 1: Protest Signs

Supplies:
The Protest signs
Handheld Musical Instruments (Optional).

Overview for Leader:
In this lesson, the children have seen, heard, talked, and created things about resistance. The action of marching together will help reinforce what they have learned.

Repeated Ideas for Lesson 4 "I Am Resistant":
- Resistance means to stand firm against something, and for the purpose of these lessons, it means to not participate in unfairness or unkindness, to stand firm against those things.
- Resisting unfairness is a way to help the world become better and more fair, like God intended.

Introductory Statement: Sometimes, things need to be changed in the world. Dr. Martin Luther King said, "Injustice anywhere is a threat to justice everywhere." When we see injustice or unfairness, we can't go along with it. Everyone can do something. Even children can resist.

Instructions: Once the signs are finished, have the children practice marching holding their signs. Those adults who did not make signs can play instruments as they march (optional). Additionally, you can create chants/cheers, to say as you march. If you coordinate with your church, you could even plan a protest march on your church campus or some other traffic-free location and invite others from your church to participate. Or you could hold or leave some of the signs up in the parking lot or along the road for others to see as they drive by, if that makes sense for your location.

Summary Statement (summarize main idea of activity & connect to the theme):
Resistance means taking a stand against something, as we have discussed in our lessons for us it means to not participate in unfairness or unkindness. When we resist unfairness, we help the world become a better place, as God intended.

Option 2: Letter Writing

Supplies:
Paper and writing utensils
OR photocopies of a prepared letter that the children can decorate
Stamps

Overview for Leader:
In this lesson, the children have seen, heard, talked, and created things about resistance. This part may take some advanced planning. If possible, the ideal would be to ask the children about messes or problems they want to work on fixing in the world, and then do some research about letter writing campaigns related to those problems. There are probably already organizations that are doing work around justice in many areas, including your local area. Finding one that is already doing the work to add your voices to teaches partnership and often is more effective. Doing some advanced research on organizations committed to justice in your area would be helpful, especially if it is related to particular problems the participants want to work on.

Repeated Ideas for Lesson 4 "I Am Resistant":
- Resistance means to stand firm against something, and for the purpose of these lessons, it means to not participate in unfairness or unkindness, to stand firm against those things.
- Resisting unfairness is a way to help the world become better and more fair, like God intended.

Introductory Statement: Sometimes, things need to be changed in the world. Dr. Martin Luther King said, "Injustice anywhere is a threat to justice everywhere." When we see injustice or unfairness, we can't go along with it. Everyone can do something. Even children can resist.

Instructions: Pass out paper and writing utensils or decoration supplies. Explain that they are going to be speaking up to resist the unfairness they see by writing a letter to leaders who are working on that problem, and they are adding their voices to let it be known to the world they hope to create and live in. Explain a bit more about the specific campaign or organization they're writing to. Children can draw pictures of the world they want to live in or write about what they don't like about the problem they see, and what they hope will change.

Summary Statement (summarize main idea of activity & connect to the theme): Resistance means taking a stand against something; as we have discussed in our lessons, for us it means to not participate in unfairness or unkindness. When we resist unfairness, we help the world become a better place, as God intended. Today you spoke up to resist unfairness and helped start creating the world God dreamed of.

Lesson/Day 5: I Am Ready

- Theme: Take Action
- Main Idea: We are the hands and feet of Christ (St. Teresa of Avila)
- Explanation/Teaching Approach: As God's hands and feet in the world, it's our job to help God realize God's dream for the world. Examples of actions we can take are: when things are unfair, make them right (don't leave it a mess); when people are left out, include them.

Objectives:
- To understand that we can take action to help work on problems in the world now; we don't have to wait for others to do it
- To value taking action by brainstorming problems that they want to fix and ways they might go about making the world better
- To practice serving and helping when we see needs, especially through the service project

Elements:
1. Bible Story: James 2 (take action, and don't play favorites; be fair to everyone)
2. Story Book:
   a. *The Three Questions* by Jon J. Muth (concrete examples of actions that can help)
   b. *One Plastic Bag* by Miranda Paul (one person can start something that makes a big difference)
   c. *Something Happened in Our Town* by Marianne Celano, Marietta Collins, and Ann Hazzard (understanding of other perspectives, inclusive of new people)
3. Personal Story: Children making a difference. Examples:
   a. Building shelters for those experiencing homelessness
   b. Growing food for those who are hungry/community gardens
   c. Collecting art supplies for kids in foster care
   d. Making blankets for kids who need extra love
4. Art (hands and feet of Christ)
   a. Flip Flop Art
   b. Hands
   c. Decorate St. Teresa poem

5. Music: "With My Own Two Hands" by Ben Harper
6. Play/Activity
    a. With one person behind another, the back person acts as the front person's hands to complete a task (make a sandwich or finish a 10-piece puzzle)
    b. Other teamwork games
7. Snack:
    a. Decorate a foot-shaped cookie (verse: how beautiful are the feet of those who bring good news, and we have good news to share, that with God's help, we can work to make the world like God's dream)
    b. Lady fingers (hands and feet in the world)
8. Serve/Do:
    a. Support a refugee resettlement agency, or together with your church help resettle a refugee family.
    b. Have a money jar to collect whatever coins each child can send every day (for every coin they get a raffle ticket for a big stuffed animal).

Introduction to Lesson and Theme

Theme: Take Action
Main Idea: We are the hands and feet of Christ (St. Teresa of Avila)

Upfront Illustration: Being the "Hands"
Use the activity for today and have leaders do the activity up front (children will have a chance to do this themselves during the activity time).

Introduce the Main Ideas (say something like):
God created us all with so much love. God created us different from each other because it shows something about how amazing God is. God dreamed of a world where everyone would be treated with love. But human beings often treat those they see as different with unkindness. We messed up God's dream. So, God sent Jesus to show us how to treat people with love, to try to bring God's dream to earth. Jesus showed us amazing things! Jesus loved everyone, served everyone, took care of people, had compassion, and helped them.

When Jesus rose from the dead and then ascended back into heaven, the work of showing the world God's dream was left to us! As God's hands and feet in the world, it's our job to help God realize God's dream for the world. Examples of actions we can take are: when things are unfair, make them right (don't leave it a mess); when people are left out, include them.

Now that we've learned more about what God intended for the world, plus some of the things that are a mess and how the world needs help, we can get to working on it!

Repeated Ideas:
- WE are the ones God has asked to do the work. It's up to us. God will help.
- We are ready to take action! We are loved. We are brave. We are compassionate. We can resist the ways the world doesn't do it right.
- We have feet to go to where the needs are. We have hands to serve. We have hearts to love. We can do it!

Bible Story 5 | James 2

Scripture Reference: James 2:1-4, 8-9, 14-17

My brothers and sisters, believers in our glorious Lord Jesus Christ must not show favoritism. Suppose a man comes into your meeting wearing a gold ring and fine clothes, and a poor man in filthy old clothes also comes in. If you show special attention to the man wearing fine clothes and say, "Here's a good seat for you," but say to the poor man, "You stand there" or "Sit on the floor by my feet," have you not discriminated among yourselves and become judges with evil thoughts?

If you really keep the royal law found in Scripture, "Love your neighbor as yourself," you are doing right. But if you show favoritism, you sin and are convicted by the law as lawbreakers.

What good is it, my brothers and sisters, if someone claims to have faith but has no deeds? Can such faith save them? Suppose a brother or a sister is without clothes and daily food. If one of you says to them, "Go in peace; keep warm and well fed," but does nothing about their physical needs, what good is it? In the same way, faith by itself, if it is not accompanied by action, is dead.

Supplies/Set-Up:
- Brainstorm in advance and be ready with some situations children might find themselves in where someone is treated unfairly (like if one child is excluded from playing a game, or if they see someone sitting alone, or if one child is making fun of how another child's name sounds, or if they are saying anything negative about their physical appearance or abilities).

Overview for Leaders: The main goal of this section is to help them prepare for some situations they might find themselves in (or have already found themselves in before) where someone is being treated unfairly, and to help the children practice doing something about unfairness when they see it. They'll do this in the form of skits. For younger children, you may need to have some ideas of unfairness and a good response to it ready for them to act out. Older children can come up with their own.

Repeated Ideas for Lesson 5 "I Am Ready":
- WE are the ones God has asked to do the work. It's up to us. God will help.
- We are ready to take action! We are loved. We are brave. We are compassionate. We can resist the ways the world doesn't do it right.
- We have feet to go to where the needs are. We have hands to serve. We have hearts to love. We can do it!

Storytelling Technique:
- Talk through some of the main ideas:
  - Favoritism is when we don't treat everyone fairly; instead, we treat some people as better than other people.
  - Every person is made in God's image, and we should treat them all with goodness and kindness; all of them, rich or poor, have the goodness of God in them. We have to treat everyone fairly with goodness and kindness.
  - If we have faith in God, and we really believe that every single person is made in God's image, and that there is goodness in every single person, then we will ACT on that belief. We will DO something. James tells us that if we see that someone, a fellow human being who is made in God's image, has a need, then we will take action to meet that need. That's what true faith is.
- Divide the children into groups of about 5.
- Children will make a short skit. Instruct them to think of a time in real life when someone has been treated unfairly or when someone has had a need. Have them act out what they would do to help in the unfair situation or to help in meeting that need. (Examples might be: someone who is left out and how to include them, standing up for someone who is being made fun of, kids who are saying someone's name wrong and how to teach that it's important to get it right, someone who needs help, such as a new student at school who needs help learning how things work in a new place).
- Give them a few minutes to plan and practice and then have them present their short skits.

"Wondering" Questions:
I wonder what it would be like to step into those situations that were unfair and try to help? Or to help meet someone's need? What might make you nervous? What might feel good? I wonder how the person who was treated unfairly or had a need might feel when we step in to help? I wonder what the world would be like if everyone always stepped in to help?

Summary Statement (summarize main idea & connect back to theme):
- WE are the ones God has asked to do the work. It's up to us. God will help.
- We are ready to take action! We are loved. We are brave. We are compassionate. We can resist the ways the world doesn't do it right.
- We have feet to go to where the needs are. We have hands to serve. We have hearts to love. We can do it!

Story Book 5

There are several options here that show examples of ways we can take action to make the world a better place. *The Three Questions* might be more appropriate for younger children with concrete examples of seeing a need and helping. *One Plastic Bag* shows how one person, starting small, made a big difference in the world. *Something Happened in Our Town* is about the police shooting of an unarmed person of color and families who are helping their children to process that. It ends with a concrete example of inclusion that helps bridge division.

Option 1: *The Three Questions* (Pre-K/K and up)

Overview for Leader: *The Three Questions*, based on a story by Leo Tolstoy, follows a boy on a journey to discover how to be a good person by asking three questions: When is the best time to do things? Who is the most important one? and What is the right thing to do? As he tries to answer his question, he encounters animal friends that need help and learns that now is the best time to do things, the person you are with is the most important one, and to do best for whoever is by your side is the right thing to do.

Repeated Ideas for Lesson 5 "I Am Ready":
- WE are the ones God has asked to do the work. It's up to us. God will help.
- We are ready to take action! We are loved. We are brave. We are compassionate. We can resist the ways the world doesn't do it right.
- We have feet to go to where the needs are. We have hands to serve. We have hearts to love. We can do it!

Introductory Statement: This is a story about a little boy that wants to do good, but he gets caught up in the details of how to make that happen. While trying to decide how to be a good person, he goes on a journey where he meets several friends that help him figure out the best way to be a good person and do the right thing.

Read the Story: *The Three Questions* [Based on a Story by Leo Tolstoy] by Jon J. Muth, Scholastic Press, 2002

"Wondering" Questions:
- I wonder how it felt for Nikolai to help those animals. Was he scared? Excited? Did the work make him tired?

- I wonder if the animals would have gotten the help they needed if Nikolai hadn't been there. Would they have been okay? Would someone else have come by to help?
- I wonder what I would have done if I had met those animals when they needed help. Would I have noticed they needed help? Would I have had time to help? Would I have been strong or brave enough?
- I wonder how often the people around me need help. Do I take time to notice them? Can I do hard things to help other people?

Summary Statement (summarize main idea of story & connect back to theme):
God has asked all of us to help do the work of caring for each other. Sometimes, like Nikolai did, we can spend a lot of time wondering what we should do or who we should help, but really, God has asked us to do whatever we can, whenever we can! When we are both big and small, all we have to do is look around us for people who need help, and then do the best we can to help them. All of those acts of love make God happy.

Option 2: *One Plastic Bag* (elementary)

Overview for Leader:
This story is about how one person saw a problem (plastic bags were killing livestock and hurting the environment) and mobilized a group of women to do something about it. It is the true story of how they used the plastic to crochet purses and bags they sold, and how they made a difference for the better in the world.

Repeated Ideas for Lesson 5 "I Am Ready":
- WE are the ones God has asked to do the work. It's up to us. God will help.
- We are ready to take action! We are loved. We are brave. We are compassionate. We can resist the ways the world doesn't do it right.
- We have feet to go to where the needs are. We have hands to serve. We have hearts to love. We can do it!

Introductory Statement:
Did you know that one person can make a big difference? We're going to read a story about how one woman made a huge difference in her area. She saw a problem, and she knew she could do something about it. So she did. She saw the need, and she took action to do something about it!

Read the Story: *One Plastic Bag: Isatou Ceesay and the Recycling Women of Gambia* by Miranda Paul, illustrated by Elizabeth Zunon, Millbrook Press, 2015

"Wondering" Questions:
- When you heard about the problem with the plastic bags in the beginning of this story, I wonder what ideas you had to help fix that problem? I wonder what you thought of Isatou's idea at first…did you think it would work? Crocheting plastic like you would crochet with yarn?
- I wonder what it must have been like with others doubting you, and maybe you also doubting yourself, wondering whether your idea would actually help? I wonder why Isatou didn't give up? It seems like such a big problem! Like maybe it would never be fixed. Like maybe one person couldn't do anything that would make a difference!
- I wonder what those other women saw that convinced them to help Isatou even though they weren't sure if it would work?
- I wonder what problems you see in the world that you would like to help fix?

Summary Statement (summarize main idea of story & connect back to theme):
The problem caused by the plastic bags and garbage was causing livestock to die, people to get sick, and the environment to be damaged. It was a huge problem, one Isatou could easily have tried to keep ignoring, and hoping someone else would fix. But WE are the ones who are called to do the work to help fix the world. And one person can make a huge difference, just like Isatou is doing. She had help, but she's the one who started it! When we see a problem or a mess, WE are the ones God has asked to do the work. It's up to us. And God will help. We are ready to take action! We are loved. We are brave. We are compassionate. We can resist the ways the world doesn't do it right. We have feet to go to where the needs are. We have hands to serve. We have hearts to love. We can do it!

Option 3: *Something Happened in Our Town* (elementary)

Overview for Leader: Something Happened in Our Town is about the police shooting of an unarmed person of color, and families who are helping their children to process that. It ends with a concrete example of inclusion that helps bridge division.

Repeated Ideas for Lesson 5 "I Am Ready":
- WE are the ones God has asked to do the work. It's up to us. God will help.
- We are ready to take action! We are loved. We are brave. We are compassionate. We can resist the ways the world doesn't do it right.
- We have feet to go to where the needs are. We have hands to serve. We have hearts to love. We can do it!

Introductory Statement:
This story is about something unfair that happened, and there are two kids who heard about it; they are talking about it with their parents so they can try to understand it. What they learn helps them do the right thing when a new student comes to their class.

Read the Story: *Something Happened in Our Town: A Child's Story about Racial Injustice* by Marianne Celano, Marietta Collins, and Ann Hazzard, illustrated by Jennifer Zivoin, Magination Press, 2018

"Wondering" Questions:
- I wonder if you've ever noticed unfairness happening? Or even patterns of unfairness? I wonder if you've ever heard of something like that unfairness happening in your town?
- I wonder where you found hope in this story?
- I wonder if you've ever been the one who was left out like Omad? I wonder if you've ever been the one who invited people to come in like Emma and Josh? I wonder if you ever had to stand up for someone and insist that they be included like Josh?
- I wonder how else you and I can take action to include people and make sure we are not separated from each other?

Summary Statement (summarize main idea of story & connect back to theme):
Emma and Josh made a huge difference in the new student, Omad's, life. They took action to make him feel welcome and a part of their group. They made the world a more fair and loving place because they stood up for him. They noticed what he was going through. They saw him with compassion so they could imagine what he might be feeling and what he might

need; they resisted and didn't go along with their classmates who tried to leave him out, and they took action to invite him in. We can do that too! We are ready to take action. We have eyes to see what people need, we have feet to go to where the needs are, we have hands to serve, and hearts to love! We can do it!

Personal Story 5 | Children Making a Difference

Overview for Leader: When we are young, sometimes we can fall into the trap of believing that we will start doing important things when we are older. But the truth is, anyone who understands that something needs to be done can find a way to be helpful. We are ALL equipped to take action and serve the world in love as God calls us to. There are several options for the personal story in today's lesson because there are so many young people who are doing amazing things to set the world right. Choose the stories that you think your group will connect with the best.

Repeated Ideas for Lesson 5 "I Am Ready":
- WE are the ones God has asked to do the work. It's up to us. God will help.
- We are ready to take action! We are loved. We are brave. We are compassionate. We can resist the ways the world doesn't do it right.
- We have feet to go to where the needs are. We have hands to serve. We have hearts to love. We can do it!

Introductory Statement: One person can make a huge difference. Children can make a big difference in the world too! Remember that previously, we learned the stories of Ruby Bridges and Audrey Faye Hendricks, who were children, and changed the world with the ways they resisted unfairness. Their experiences happened several decades ago, but children are still making a difference in the world, and you can too! God has prepared YOU to make a difference. You have eyes of compassion to see the needs, feet to go where the needs are, hands to serve, and hearts to love, and you can make a difference in the world, just like these children!

Show video(s):

Choose one or more stories of children changing the world. You can find articles and videos about these children in the Resources section of the Diocese of Atlanta website (go to Resources > Education and Formation > Dismantling Racism Curriculum Resources).

- William's Weekend for Backpack Buddies: An 8-year-old boy in North Carolina has collected hundreds of pounds of food to feed the hungry in his county.
- Chelsea's charity (art supplies for foster kids)
- Lucy's Love Blankets (makes blankets for kids who need some extra love)
- Duck and Chick (two sisters who make really cool leather goods and donate the money to Heifer International)
- Hailey's Harvest (a 9-year-old girl built homeless shelters and started a garden to feed the hungry)

Summary Statement (summarize main idea of story & connect back to theme):
- WE are the ones God has asked to do the work. It's up to us. God will help.
- We are ready to take action! We are loved. We are brave. We are compassionate. We can resist the ways the world doesn't do it right.
- We have feet to go to where the needs are. We have hands to serve. We have hearts to love. We can do it!

Art 5

Option 1: Flip Flop Art

Supplies:
- Inexpensive plastic/rubber flip flops. One pair for each child.
- Paints, brushes, and/or paint pens

Overview for Leader:
Today's main focus is to learn how we are called to take action and be the hands and FEET of God. In this activity, the children will remember the ways that they can take action and turn a pair of flip flops into art that remind them to do the work they have been called to do.

Repeated Ideas for Lesson 5 "I Am Ready":
- WE are the ones God has asked to do the work. It's up to us. God will help.
- We are ready to take action! We are loved. We are brave. We are compassionate. We can resist the ways the world doesn't do it right.
- We have feet to go to where the needs are. We have hands to serve. We have hearts to love. We can do it!

Introductory Statement: These past few days (weeks) we have been talking about how to do the work of fixing the messes we have made and help restore God's dream for us. We can all play a role and be brave enough to do our part of the work. As you think about the role you might play, what comes to mind? How might those things be expressed in art? Let's take some time to create a piece of art that will remind us that God uses us and our bodies to make the work happen.

Instructions:
- Remind the children of some of the main teaching points of the day, focusing on how we are called to take action by being the FEET of God.
- Ask them to share some of the ways that they specifically can take action to share God's love, fix messes, and make things closer to God's dream for us.
- Pass out the supplies and invite the children to decorate the flip flops with words, shapes, and symbols that remind them of the things they want to do to take action.
- Give them time to share their creations with the group!

Summary Statement (summarize main idea of art & connect back to the theme):
As you wear these flip flops out into the world, they will remind you that God has invited you to be a part of God's story by taking action to love each other and fix messes. Share the meaning with friends and family, pray when you take note of your flip flops, and enjoy the work God is inviting you to participate in!

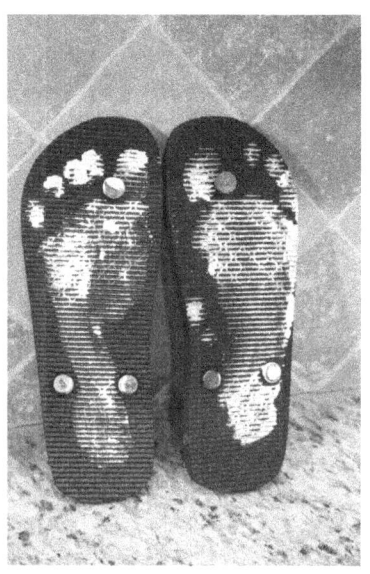

Option 2: Handprint Art

Supplies:
- Colorful, thick paper
- Markers
- Scissors
- Other possible decorating items: glitter and glue, stickers, sequins, etc.

Overview for Leader:
Today's main focus is to learn about how we are called to take action and be the HANDS and feet of God. In this activity, the children will remember the ways that they can take action and decorate a cut-out of their hand to remind them to do the work they have been called to do.

Repeated Ideas for Lesson 5 "I Am Ready":
- WE are the ones God has asked to do the work. It's up to us. God will help.
- We are ready to take action! We are loved. We are brave. We are compassionate. We can resist the ways the world doesn't do it right.
- We have feet to go to where the needs are. We have hands to serve. We have hearts to love. We can do it!

Introductory Statement: These past few days (weeks) we have been talking about how to do the work of fixing the messes we have made and help restore God's dream for us. We can all play a role and be brave enough to do our part of the work. As you think about the role you might play, what comes to mind? How might those things be expressed in art? Let's take some time to create a piece of art that will remind us that God uses us and our bodies to make the work happen.

Instructions:
- Remind the children of some of the main teaching points of the day, focusing on how we are called to take action by being the HANDS of God.
- Ask them to share some of the ways that they specifically can take action to share God's love, fix messes, and make things closer to God's dream for us.
- Pass out the supplies and invite the children to trace their hand and cut it out of the paper. (HINT: For younger children or if you have limited time, you may want to cut out shapes of hands before the children arrive.)
- Then they can decorate their "hands" with words, shapes, and symbols that remind them of the things they want to do to take action.

- Give them time to share their creations with the group!
- BONUS: You've likely seen people take many cut-out hands and arrange them to make one larger shape like a heart, cross, or tree. If you would like to have a piece of collaborative art to share with the entire church, this would be a wonderful opportunity to collect their work and turn it into a single piece.

Summary Statement (summarize main idea of art, and connect back to the theme):
We all have different hands and different roles we can take in being the hands of God in this world. As you look at the hand you created, be reminded of how you have been called to take action and love those around you!

Option 3: St. Teresa of Avila Poem Decorated

Supplies:
- Printed copies St. Teresa of Avila "Christ Has No Body" poems, 1/child
- Nice, thicker colorful paper to serve as a backing; lots of different ones to choose from
- Small things to decorate with:
  - Stickers or pictures of hands, feet, eyes, hearts
  - Puff balls, feathers, glitter, glitter glue, pipe cleaners, whatever you have on hand
  - Glue

Overview for Leader: This poem by St. Teresa of Avila pulls together some of the themes of Lesson 1, about being the Body of Christ, and how everyone is needed to work together. This poem also tells us that God is calling US to be partners to do the work on earth.

Repeated Ideas for Lesson 5 "I Am Ready":
- WE are the ones God has asked to do the work. It's up to us. God will help.
- We are ready to take action! We are loved. We are brave. We are compassionate. We can resist the ways the world doesn't do it right.
- We have feet to go to where the needs are. We have hands to serve. We have hearts to love. We can do it!

Introductory Statement: In several of our lessons, we've talked about how human beings sometimes mess things up and treat each other with unkindness, and it makes a mess. God could just fix it right now, but God doesn't choose to do that. I wonder why that might be? Why might God not just fix everything and make them perfect right now? *(pause for discussion)*. I'm not sure we 100% know the answer to that, but maybe we've got some ideas. What I do know is that God invites us to partner with God to put the world back together. We are God's hands and feet in this world. St. Teresa of Avila wrote a beautiful poem about how we are the ones who get to do the work to help make the world better. If anything needs to be done in the world, WE are the ones who can do it, and God will give us everything we need to do that work. We are ready, and today we'll decorate this beautiful poem to remind us that it's US! We are the ones who can put the world back together and make a difference, with God's help!

Instructions:
- Each child will get a printed poem and can choose a "back" (nicer, thick, colorful piece of paper).

- In bowls, put supplies and glue at each table.
- Glue the poem to the back.
- Glue decorations around.
- Let dry.
- As children are creating, adults can sit at each table and ask questions (and share stories) like:
    - What are some things you do with your hands that serve others?
    - What are some places your feet take you to, where you can help others?
    - When you look at others, I wonder what you see; when you look with your compassion glasses do you see them how God sees them, as wonderful and beloved? What are some wonderful things about those around you?
    - What are some ways you have been loving to others?

Summary Statement (summarize main idea of art & connect back to the theme):
God has given us the task of taking action to help this world be better, and we are ready! We have feet to go to where the needs are, we have hands to serve, we have eyes to see with compassion, we have hearts to love. We are ready!

Christ Has No Body
Christ has no body but yours,
No hands, no feet on earth but yours,
Yours are the eyes with which he looks
Compassion on this world,
Yours are the feet with which he walks to do good,
Yours are the hands, with which he blesses all the world.
Yours are the hands, yours are the feet,
Yours are the eyes, you are his body.
Christ has no body now but yours,
No hands, no feet on earth but yours,
Yours are the eyes with which he looks
compassion on this world.
Christ has no body now on earth but yours.
Teresa of Avila (1515–1582)

Music 5

"With My Own Two Hands"

<u>Song #1</u>: "With My Own Two Hands," by Ben Harper, performed with Jack Johnson. You can find and purchase sheet music online.

Overview for Leader: There are several versions of "With My Own Two Hands, " but the version performed by Jack Johnson and Ben Harper is probably the best fit for children.

Repeated Ideas for Lesson 5 "I Am Ready":
- WE are the ones God has asked to do the work. It's up to us. God will help.
- We are ready to take action! We are loved. We are brave. We are compassionate. We can resist the ways the world doesn't do it right.
- We have feet to go to where the needs are. We have hands to serve. We have hearts to love. We can do it!

Introductory Statement to Singing the Song: We know there are so many things to be done to restore things to the way God intended. We also know that we have what it takes, right now, to do some of that work. As we sing this song, think about the ways that you can change the world for God's glory with your own two hands.

Special Instructions /Motions:
Have children act out the lyrics, like comforting others or cleaning the earth. Have them hold up their hands whenever it says "with my own two hands" or invite them to help create motions.

Summary Statement (summarize main idea & connect back to the theme):
It can sometimes be hard for both adults and children to find practical ways to make this world a better place, but this song is essentially a list of ways to do just that. I wonder about which actions would be most natural for you? Which ones would challenge you? What are some other ways that you can use your own two hands to make the world a better place? I wonder how God might feel when we perform some of these actions?

<u>**Song #2**</u>: "Go Serve Our World" by Yancy

This song is licensed under CCLI licensing. Lyrics and more can also be found at the Yancy Ministries website.

Overview for Leader: This song is often used in VBS, and the words go along with the theme of this lesson about taking action and serving others.

Repeated Ideas for Lesson 5 "I Am Ready":
- WE are the ones God has asked to do the work. It's up to us. God will help.
- We are ready to take action! We are loved. We are brave. We are compassionate. We can resist the ways the world doesn't do it right.
- We have feet to go to where the needs are. We have hands to serve. We have hearts to love. We can do it!

Introductory Statement to Singing the Song: We are the ones who are called to take action to make this world better. This is God's world, and God entrusted us to care for it and all the people in it too. We have eyes to see the needs, feet to go to where the needs are, hands to serve, and hearts to love. We can serve our world and make a difference, and this song is a reminder to go and serve!

Special Instructions/Motions:
This song has been choreographed before. If you search for Go Serve Our World VBS Song, you'll find some examples. Or you can have the children create their own motions.

Summary Statement (summarize main idea & connect back to the theme):
It's up to us! We are the ones who are called to take action and make a difference, and we are ready! We have what we need. We have eyes to see the needs, feet to go to where the needs are, hands to serve, and hearts to love! We can do it!

Play/Activity 5

Supplies:
Bread
Sandwich supplies: Mayo, mustard, hummus, slices of turkey, cheese
Plastic Knives
Blindfold (optional)

LEADER TIP: Other ideas for tasks to complete (which would require different supplies): dress a doll or color a picture.

Overview for Leader: The point of this activity is to illustrate what it might look like to be God's hands in the world, to give some insight about how God might work through us to accomplish the task God has called us to: to partner with God to put the world back together and to make God's dream for us a reality. We are the ones who can do it, and God is with us to direct us and help us and show us how, but we are the ones to do this work! Again, when using analogies and illustrations, the jump between concrete (physically being the hands to make a sandwich) to abstract (how we can be the "hands" by serving others in the world) requires some careful and intentional verbal bridges.

Repeated Ideas for Lesson 5 "I Am Ready":
- WE are the ones God has asked to do the work. It's up to us. God will help.
- We are ready to take action! We are loved. We are brave. We are compassionate. We can resist the ways the world doesn't do it right.
- We have feet to go to where the needs are. We have hands to serve. We have hearts to love. We can do it!

Introductory Statement:
We've talked about how we are ready to take action, how we are God's hands and feet in the world. God is asking US to take action. Sure, God can do anything, with or without us, but USUALLY God chooses to work THROUGH us, meaning God chooses US to do the work that needs to be done in the world. Our work that God calls us to is bringing God's dream to the world, God's dream of where everyone is treated with love. But today, we're going to do some other work…we're going to make a sandwich. So, one volunteer is going to be God, and have the knowledge of the work that needs to be done and what it should look like when it's finished, and can talk and guide and direct. The other volunteer is going

to be the hands, the one who can actually touch all the things and get the task done (but can't see anything).

Instructions:

- Children will play a game requiring them to work together. One child will act as the hands. The other child will be like God, directing the Hands in the world to do the work of completing the task. God is the brain and can talk. The other child is the hands and can do what God is guiding to be done.
- God: stands in front and can see. God puts arms behind his/her/their back.
- The Hands: stands behind God with their arms out to God's side. They will be God's arms for this activity. This child is blindfolded (challenge by choice. If blindfolding is an issue, they can stay behind the other child and close their eyes so they can't see).
- Place the sandwich-making supplies on the table in front of God and Hands.
- Instruct God to guide the hands to make a sandwich, using only words.
- Instruct the Hands to listen to what God is saying as God directs them to make a sandwich.

Debrief/Discussion:

I wonder what was hard about that? I wonder what was easy?

If God often chooses US to be the hands, the ones doing the work, I wonder if we are good listeners to God when God is trying to guide us to serve or be kind or be loving? I wonder how we could be better listeners to God's guidance? I wonder why God chooses to include us in doing the work?

Summary Statement (summarize main idea of activity & connect back to the theme):
Sometimes, it seems it might be easier for God to just do the work God's self, without asking us to help. But then we wouldn't have the joy of helping to make the world better! Not that it's always a joy working on fixing this world…it's hard work, but it certainly is an important and meaningful job to do, and God has asked us to do it! God has given us what we need to do that work. We have feet to go to where people have needs, hands to serve, eyes to see with compassion, and hearts to love. God chooses US to be a part of this important work, and we are READY to do it!

Snack 5 | Foot Cookies

Supplies:
- Foot cookies (you can order these already made from places like Etsy online, or you can make them in advance with foot cookie cutters)
- Cookie icing to spread over the cookie
- Sprinkles of lots of different colors, shapes, sizes
- Edible baking decorations of all kinds
- Colored icing in tubes to write with
- Print up cards with | "How beautiful are the feet of those who bring Good News" —Isaiah 52:7 | and place at tables.

Overview for Leader: This snack reminds us that we are God's feet in the world. We are the ones who do things in the world like bring the Good News that God is love and has a beautiful dream for the world that we're all invited into, and that God is putting the world back together by showing us how to love, especially through Jesus. Scripture says that those who bring Good News have beautiful feet, so children will decorate a foot cookie and make it look beautiful to remind us that we are the ones who need to walk around this world and take action and spread the Good News about God's love.

Repeated Ideas for Lesson 5 "I Am Ready":
- WE are the ones God has asked to do the work. It's up to us. God will help.
- We are ready to take action! We are loved. We are brave. We are compassionate. We can resist the ways the world doesn't do it right.
- We have feet to go to where the needs are. We have hands to serve. We have hearts to love. We can do it!

Introductory Statement:
We are God's hands and feet in the world. If God wants to act, God often chooses to have US act in the world as God would act in the world. Scripture says "How beautiful are the feet of the one who brings Good News" (Isaiah 52:7). I don't know if I've ever really thought of feet as beautiful, but the Bible says that the ones who run to tell Good News have beautiful feet! I wonder if we could have beautiful feet….do we have any Good News we can tell others? What are some things we've been learning about this week that might be Good News to share? *(God loves us all, God has a beautiful dream where everyone is loved, we can help make the world a better place with God's help… that's all Good News!)* When we share that Good News that God loves us and wants to create a loving world, and we can help… when we run to tell everyone that Good News, God says that to God, our feet sure do look beautiful when

we are running to tell everyone that! So, we're going to decorate some feet *(show cookie)* to remind us that our feet look beautiful to God when we are doing God's work in the world and sharing the Good News that God loves everyone!

Instructions:
- Pass out one cookie on a plate to each child.
- Put bowls of supplies on the table to share.
- Spread icing (let children do this or help if needed) over the cookie so everything will stick to it.
- Let children add their sprinkles or other decorations of their choice.
- With tubes of icing, they may want to write Isaiah 52:7, if desired.

Summary Statement (summarize main idea & connect back to the theme):

We are ready to share some Good News of things we've learned! That God loves us, that God has a beautiful dream for us and this world, and that we can help God bring that dream to the world. We are ready to take action. We have hands to serve, feet to go and tell people, eyes to see with compassion, and hearts to love. We are ready to go and help! And when you do that, God thinks your feet sure do look pretty, because you're using them to help others!

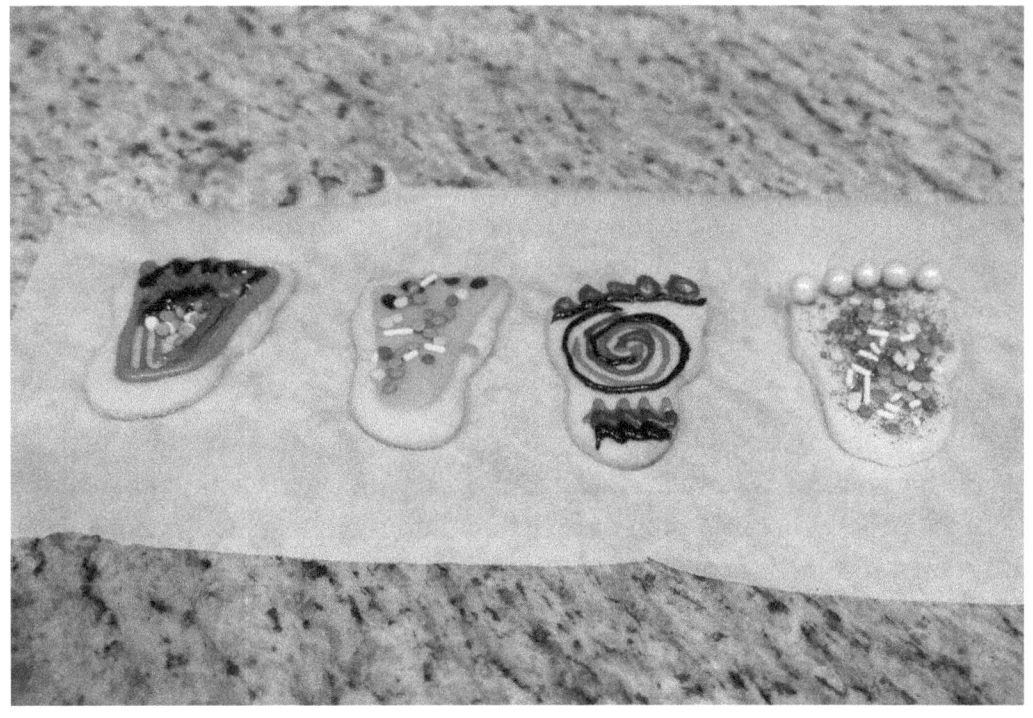

Serve/Do 5 | Support Refugees

Option 1: Raffle Fundraiser

Supplies:
- Raffle tickets
- Large Bowl
- Refugee-made stuffed animal (you can find one at the Preemptive Love Coalition's website), along with possible other fun things
- Huge jar to collect coins and bills
- pens/pencils

Overview for Leader: This activity can be introduced at the beginning of the lesson series and continue throughout the series. At the end of the series, you'll raffle off the prize, and you'll also announce how much money you've raised for a refugee resettlement agency (or other non-profit helping the marginalized that you might choose).

Repeated Ideas for Lesson 5 "I Am Ready":
- WE are the ones God has asked to do the work. It's up to us. God will help.
- We are ready to take action! We are loved. We are brave. We are compassionate. We can resist the ways the world doesn't do it right.
- We have feet to go to where the needs are. We have hands to serve. We have hearts to love. We can do it!

Introductory Statement: We've been working all along to take action, and one way we did that was to collect money each and every time you came for a lesson, so thank you for your donations! They are going to go toward helping a refugee family get settled here and set up with a home.

Instructions:
Encourage the children to bring any coins or bills each day of the lessons to donate to an agency that helps refugees. Give each child a raffle ticket and have them write their name on it and add it to the bowl. For each coin or bill, the children can write their name on an additional raffle ticket and add it to the bowl. At the end of the lesson series, a drawing will held to determine the winner of the refugee-made toys.

Summary Statement (summarize main idea of activity & connect to the theme): God has called us to take action, and we have! This is just one way we've made a difference in the world and to a family. And we can keep making a difference in LOTS of ways! We are ready!

Option 2: Help Resettle a Refugee Family

Instructions:
- Research organizations that help refugees in your own area. If there is a refugee resettlement agency, reach out about partnering with them to resettle an incoming refugee family. They often need donations of furniture, bedding, toys/books/games for children, and personal items that make a new place feel more like a home.
- Organize a drive to furnish a refugee home by collecting needed items.
- If the refugee resettlement agency resettles refugees near your area, you might also arrange for volunteers to visit the family, invite them to church, help them run errands, etc.
- You can ask the children what makes them feel most at home and ask them to bring something for refugee children that would make them feel more at home.
- You can also have the children make cards for families with well-wishes and prayers.

Wrap-Up

At the end of the series, don't forget to revisit, celebrate, and update the group on these elements:

1. Quilt: Display the quilt that was created at the beginning of the series and remind children that we are all unique and beautiful as individuals, but even more so when we come together as one! Together, we provide the world with something amazing!
2. Pictures: You might also collect and display pictures of the children participating in the series (make sure you have a media release from grown-ups allowing photography). Another idea might be to take pictures of each individual participating and use them to create a bigger image (like of the church) out of the individual portraits (illustrating a similar idea as the quilt). For examples of websites that can help you do that, visit the Diocese of Atlanta website (go to Resources > Education and Formation > Dismantling Racism Curriculum Resources).
3. Service Project: Whatever service project you choose to do, be sure to provide an update on where things are, what has been done, what has been generously received already, what is still needed, the impact of the project, etc.
4. Children's stories: If possible, collect quotes from the children on what they have learned and what it has meant to them, and share them with the congregation (you may want to seek permission from the responsible adults). You might even do this via video.
5. Shared Meal: One way to celebrate the end of the series might be to have a shared meal. If you have people in your congregation who are from countries other than the United States, you might ask them to make and bring a dish to share from their countries of origin, perhaps with a note telling about the dish. You might also report on the service project and share quotes/video of quotes or have children share about their experiences at this celebration meal.

Living God's Dream

www.ingramcontent.com/pod-product-compliance
Lightning Source LLC
Chambersburg PA
CBHW081818300426
44116CB00014B/2407